THE REALITY OF THE RELIGIOUS LIFE

THE REALITY OF THE RELIGIOUS LIFE

A Study of Miracle
Providence and Prayer

HENRY BETT
M.A., Litt.D.

HODDER AND STOUGHTON
ST. PAUL'S HOUSE, WARWICK SQUARE
LONDON, E.C.4

FIRST PUBLISHED MARCH, 1949

PRINTED IN GREAT BRITAIN FOR
HODDER AND STOUGHTON LIMITED, LONDON
AT THE UNIVERSITY PRESS, ABERDEEN

TO

SYDNEY WALTON

C.B.E., M.A., B.Litt.

CONTENTS

INTRODUCTORY

It is recorded that Alexander Peden, the Scottish Covenanter, was once on the moors with a company of fugitives who were being pursued by the soldiers. They reached the crest of a hill, and Peden said, "Let us pray here: for if the Lord hear not our prayers, and save us, we are all dead men". Then he prayed, "Lord, it is Thy enemy's day, hour, and power: they may not be idle. But hast Thou no other work for them, but to send them after us? Send them after them to whom Thou wilt give strength to flee, for our strength is gone. Twine them about the hill, Lord, and cast the lap of Thy cloak over Old Sandy, and thir (these) poor things, and save us this one time; and we'll keep it in remembrance, and tell it to the commendation of Thy goodness, pity and compassion, what Thou didst for us at such a time!" A cloud of mist came down between the fugitives and their pursuers, and in the meantime a messenger reached the soldiers calling them away to the pursuit of another party, who also escaped, as it was found later.[1]

That naïve story raises all the issues that are involved in the question of the supernatural, and that is why I have quoted it in preference to some Biblical miracle where the whole concern might seem to be the portent. For the supernatural, it should be remembered (though the word needs careful definition, as we shall see later) is not restricted merely to what is called miracle, but extends also to the spheres of providence and prayer, which are as vital to religion as miracle, and even more so, in the practical sense at least.

Did the incident related in the life of Peden really happen? Could it happen? Is it a record of fact, or merely a pious legend? If it happened did it come to pass as an act of God, in answer to prayer, and, if so, is it to be called a miracle? Or did it happen by the mechanical action

[1] *The Scots Worthies*, p. 510.

of natural processes, with which prayer had nothing whatever to do, and was the fact that it happened then and there a mere coincidence?

First of all, then, did the incident happen as related? That is partly a historical question, and is obviously concerned with the truthfulness of those who related it. But there is at any rate no real reason why it should not have happened, for a mist does often rise suddenly on the moors. There is nothing incredible or impossible or even improbable about that, for it occurs many times almost all the year round in the locality of which the story is told. No one need feel any difficulty in believing that such a thing did happen, and that it happened then. But many people will at once feel a real difficulty if it is suggested that the mist came in answer to Peden's prayer. The difficulty is always the same difficulty, and is always stated in much the same way. It will be said that we know in these days that the weather depends upon natural causes, and varies according to natural laws: then it will be asked, can we suppose that God interferes with these, and suspends or cancels them, in order to answer a man's prayer? That, it will be argued, would be a miracle, and the modern mind cannot accept the miraculous. All the following questions are therefore involved—What do we mean by what is possible? what is credible? what is natural? and, by consequence, what is supernatural? What do we mean by natural causes, and what determines the exceedingly complex method of their operation? What are natural laws, and what would be interference with these? In what sense is nature a mechanism? And what is a miracle? It may be difficult enough to answer some of these questions satisfactorily, but the attempt must be made, for they are all involved in the consideration of miracle and providence and prayer. There is a widely diffused notion that a modern and scientific view of the universe makes it impossible to believe in miracle, and impossible, or extremely difficult, to believe that God intervenes in an established order of events either to direct our lives or to answer our supplications—the whole idea of "intervention", as we shall see, is entirely fallacious, but that is the way it is nearly always expressed. So that most people, perhaps, in these days would at once dismiss the idea that the mist came down on the moors in answer to the Covenanter's prayer.

I want to say here, in the plainest possible terms, that though the whole question of the supernatural is beset by a mass of misunderstandings and prejudices and fallacies there is *absolutely no real reason whatever*, in science or philosophy or any other realm of human knowledge, why we should not believe that God guides our lives, and that He answers our prayers, in very strange, unforeseen and unforeseeable ways —sometimes even by what appears to be a sudden change in natural events — and that the revelation of God to men has an accompaniment of miraculous deeds. The concern of these pages is with the supposed difficulties of an intellectual kind in the way of such a conclusion. But behind all the rather abstract problems that arise there is a very practical issue. It is nothing less than the reality of religious life, for men will not long retain any real religion if they do not believe that God has revealed Himself to men in a way that is more than natural, and that He can guide and guard them by His providence on their way through life, and that He can hear and answer their earnest prayers when they cry to Him in their need.

I

THE POSSIBLE AND THE CREDIBLE

I

THE POSSIBLE AND THE CREDIBLE

WE often find that miracle, with the whole range of the supernatural in providence and prayer, is summarily dismissed as impossible. But it is very seldom that the meaning of the word has been carefully considered. What is possible, and what is not? The concept of possibility is one of the slipperiest notions with which the mind ever has to do, and it is beset with much confusion and many fallacies. First of all, it is necessary to distinguish between what may be called absolute or logical impossibility, and relative or natural impossibility. The former relates to mere contradictions in terms: it is impossible, for example, that anything should exist and not exist at the same time. Here the reference is, so to speak, to truth rather than to fact, to the realities of thought rather than to the realities of existence, or, if you prefer it, to the necessary reality of general existence as conceived in the mind rather than to the contingent realities of particular existence as found in the world. It is not a matter of particular things that might or might not exist: it is a matter of the necessary conditions that govern the general fact of existence itself. The paradox of a thing that is and is not at the same time could not even present itself in the world of fact: it could not in any way arise there. It can only present itself to the mind, and when it does so it is instantly and instinctively rejected as an impossibility. It is never an issue in reality either as a possible or as an impossible thing: to be and not to be at one and the same time is not an alternative in actuality at all, nor, as we may say, in real possibility. It can be only formulated as a mental or logical alternative, an abstraction to be at once rejected by the mind as inconceivable.

But what has been called a relative or natural impossibility is quite a different issue. We do not believe the story that St. Denys of France, after he was beheaded, walked a couple of miles carrying his head in his hands, but we do not disbelieve it on the ground of any inherent impossibility of a logical kind, as we should if the legend related that his head was both fast on his shoulders and severed in his hands at the same moment: we reject the story on the ground that the human organism, constituted as it is, does not allow muscular activity to continue for more than an instant after the brain is separated from the rest of the body. In point of fact that continuance does occur for some time in the case of some of the lower animals, and it is said that a fowl will run about and flap its wings for some moments after its head has been severed from its body. There is therefore neither any logical impossibility in the legend, nor any universal impossibility even of the natural kind, but only the particular impossibility of a particular organism acting in this particular way. What is possible for one organism is impossible for another; that is to say, what is impossible at one point or on one level of nature is possible at another. That is obvious: it is possible for a fish, and impossible for a mammal, to live under water, for example. The possibility or impossibility of any event therefore varies according to its place in the universal system of existence. Thus there is no natural impossibility of a general kind in a lost limb replacing itself by a process of growth, for that does happen with a crab, but it cannot happen with a man. The thing that is quite possible for one organism at one level of existence is quite impossible for another organism at another level.

It comes to this. We cannot state any absolute impossibility, except in the sense of a contradiction in terms. An impossibility of this logical kind may be stated, and defined beyond all doubt, as we have seen. If you say, for example, that anything cannot be in two places at the same time, it really amounts to this—a thing, that is to say, one thing, cannot be in two places at the same time, because if it could be, it would then exist as two things and not as one thing: and it is impossible for it at once both to be what it is, viz. one thing, and to be what it is not, viz. two things. In so far as the one statement is true the other statement cannot be true, and in so far as the one supposed fact is real the other supposed fact cannot be real, or there would be an end of all truth and all reality. It is the principle that reality cannot be self-contradictory and self-destructive: reality must be consistent with itself and in itself, or it would not be reality.[1]

Such impossibilities are genuine enough, but they do not concern, as it were, the impossibility of a particular fact here and there in the universe : rather they concern the necessary conditions of general existence, everywhere and always in the universe. But such impossibilities are the only impossibilities that are real and absolute. Apart from these, it cannot be said that any event that is conceivable within the structure of this universe is strictly and absolutely impossible. It may look impossible to us, because up to the present it may be entirely out of the range of our experience, and perhaps entirely out of the range of all human experience. It looks as if it never could happen, simply because it never has happened in any experience known to us. But though for that reason, it *looks* impossible, we have no right to say that it *is* impossible, strictly and ultimately, because it may yet come about in some way which is quite unimaginable to us at present. Any attempt to illustrate that supposition inevitably appears fantastic, because it is imagining what has never yet come to pass, and what therefore looks as if it never could come to pass. If I were to suggest that one day in the future, through some strange discovery, we might become aware of the existence of an order of beings in the world who had been hitherto invisible and intangible and therefore unknown to us—that suggestion would look like a fantastic impossibility. But it is not really any more strange than that within the last fifty years we should have come to know of rays that no human eye has ever seen as light, through all the uncounted ages of the past. There is nothing more impossible, in the logical and absolute sense, in the supposed discovery of the existence of invisible and

[1] Cf. A. E. Taylor, *Elements of Metaphysics*, p. 19.

intangible beings than in the actual discovery of the existence of the infra-red rays. Both alike would be the discovery of facts long accessible to our human senses, and long unsuspected by the human mind. Our estimate of the *probability* of such an imaginary discovery of unseen and unknown creatures happening as a fact would doubtless depend upon our conception of what the structure and order and purpose of the whole universe may be, and also upon our attitude to some aspects of human life and human experience, but no one can have any right whatever, on any grounds of mere rationality, to deny the *possibility* of such a thing.

What we have called logical impossibility is characterized by universal necessity of an *à priori* kind, independent, so to speak, both of detailed fact and of observation of detailed fact. It cannot be true at any time or any place that a thing that is white is black, because " white " is a contradiction in terms of " black ". That does not depend upon the actual detail that no white thing in the world *is* black, nor upon the result of observation that no white thing has even been *seen* to be black, but upon the universal necessity that no thing can be, at one and the same time, both what it is and what it is not. Every example of logical impossibility will be found, upon examination, to be a particular example of the same necessity.

We think and talk easily enough about the possible and the impossible, but as a matter of fact no one can set limits to what is possible and what is impossible, except in the logical sense that nothing can both exist and not exist at the same time. In any other sense it is impossible to define the impossible. That is quite obvious, when you think it out, and it is easy enough to illustrate it. A hundred years ago everyone would have said that it was impossible for a man in Birmingham to hear a man in London speaking. The argument would have been natural, and apparently unanswerable. The human voice, at its very loudest, cannot be heard at a greater distance than, say, half a mile to a mile. How then could it possibly be heard at a distance of more than a hundred miles ? But the telephone is invented, and then the wireless, and the thing becomes an actuality. Fifty years ago everyone would have said it was impossible for anyone to see a man's fractured rib, unless an incision in the flesh was made to expose it. Again the argument would have been quite reasonable, and apparently conclusive. Flesh is not transparent, and unless you cut through the flesh down to the bone how could anyone possibly see the fracture? But the Röntgen rays are discovered, and X-ray apparatus is found to-day in all our hospitals. There is one classical case where an eminent philosopher of the past deliberately selected and deliberately defined what he thought was a permanent impossibility. Comte declared that it would always be impossible for men to determine the chemical constitution of the fixed stars. Once again the reasoning seemed to be flawless. Since the fixed stars are millions of miles away, and since it seems impossible that men should ever leave the earth and travel through space to visit those immensely distant stars, and since without an actual visit it seems impossible to secure samples of the material of which those stars consist, and then to analyse the samples—here is something that was not merely impossible at the time when the philosopher wrote, but that would be impossible for evermore, as he thought. But not very long after Comte's day the science of spectroscopy was developed, so that we know to-day a great deal about the chemical constitution of the fixed stars. Now what has happened repeatedly in the past will undoubtedly happen again and again in the future, and what seems impossible to us to-day will become actual in the future years. But if I ventured to suggest any particular thing that seems impossible to-day as a thing that may be possible in the future it would at once look fantastic and incredible—because it is a thing that has not happened yet—exactly as the telephone, the wireless, and X-rays, and spectroscopy would have looked fantastic and incredible years before they were discovered and invented. The thing that has happened looks more possible and less wonderful than the thing that has not happened yet, because, as Kierkegaard shrewdly remarked, "We live forward; we understand backward".

There cannot be any such thing as an absolute impossibility, as we have seen, except in the sense of what has been called a logical impossibility—that is to say, some supposition which involves a contradiction in terms. Generally when we speak of anything as impossible we are referring to a relative impossibility—something which is not possible under some particular conditions, but would be possible under other conditions. Every possibility or impossibility that has any relation to the actual universe belongs to this class. It refers to something which is possible or not possible at one time, or in one place, or to one creature, or under one set of circumstances, or within one range of existence. It was not possible in the eighteenth century to travel from London to Edinburgh in an hour or two: it is possible in the twentieth century. It is not possible for palm trees to grow in the fields in Siberia: it is possible in Syria. It is not possible for a cabbage to run about the garden; it is possible for a dog. It is not possible for me, in the present state of my knowledge, to read Dostoievsky in the original; it is possible for an educated Russian. All such possibilities and impossibilities are not absolute, but *relative*—relative to some temporal, spatial, or organic facts or devices which condition the specified event, and make it, under those particular circumstances, possible or impossible. Any change in those conditions at once changes the degree of possibility and impossibility. If the aeroplane had been perfected in the eighteenth century it would have been possible to fly from London to Edinburgh in an hour or two. If the climate of the earth changed so that Siberia became a very hot country all the year round, it would be possible for palm trees to grow there. If vegetables had developed limbs and muscles in the course of evolution, in the way the animals have done, it would be possible for them to move about from place to place. If I had been born and bred and educated in Moscow it would have been possible for me to read a novel in Russian. Change some of the other facts which condition it and this particular thing which was impossible becomes possible, or equally, this particular thing which was possible becomes impossible.

That is to say, there is no inherent impossibility in any event, when considered merely in itself. It is relatively possible or impossible in respect of all that has gone before it and all that lies around it. As conditioned by the history of the past and the circumstances of the present, it may be regarded, relatively, as possible or impossible, and that is absolutely all that can be said on that particular issue of possibility. This conclusion is really another aspect of the principle stated and stressed elsewhere in these pages, that any event in the universe is the result, not of a single cause operating separately, but of an enormous grouping of causes, operating together, so that the total cause of any single event is ultimately every thing else in the universe, past and present. If the total grouping of causes at any moment had been different, the possibilities would have been different, and the thing would have happened otherwise. There is one pattern of causes in operation, and therefore this particular thing cannot happen : if the pattern of causes were changed in the past, or if it is changed now, the thing can happen. There can be no question that this is a fair statement of facts. Let the inclination of the earth's axis be changed, or let the density of the earth's atmosphere be changed, and many possible things become impossible, and impossible things possible.[2]

No one therefore has any conceivable right to declare that a miracle, or a strange providence, or a wonderful answer to prayer, is impossible. There is no question here of

[2] The quaint possibility described in the following paragraph will serve to illustrate the point. "Even a theoretically slight and simple mechanical adjustment would make us angels once again. The effect of the centrifugal force due to the earth's rotation takes off at present about $\frac{1}{289}$th part of our weight at the equator. This effect falls, of course, to zero as we move toward either pole, because we are getting nearer to the axis of rotation. If we could spin ourselves seventeen times faster this force, which varies as the square of the angular speed, would be 289 times greater and would relieve us of all our weight. We should move hither and thither at will in a so-called 'null' gravitational field, the earth's pull being completely neutralized. Instead of needing airplanes to fly from continent to continent we should effortlessly put a girdle round the earth in the manner of Shakespeare's Puck. Our babies would no longer crawl on floor or gutter but float as infant cherubs without even the need of wings." —J. M. Henry, *A New Fundamentalism*, p. 123.

logical or absolute impossibility. The possibility of it is relative to the circumstances and the period and the person concerned. What is not possible under some conditions, or at one time, or to one man, is possible under other circumstances, or in another age, or to another person. What cannot happen in normal conditions may happen in abnormal conditions. What cannot happen in one century may happen in another century. What cannot happen in my life may happen in the life of a saint. And what would be quite impossible in the acts of an ordinary man may be quite possible in the life of our Lord, if He was what His Church believes Him to be.

The supernatural is often summarily dismissed as impossible, as we have seen, but without any kind of logical warrant. With rather more plausibility, it is often classed as incredible, and dismissed on that score. But it is frequently true that an altogether arbitrary standard is assumed, and that the real canons of credibility have been thought out no better than those of possibility. What is credible, and what is not? There does not appear to be any absolute standard of credibility, with the single exception of what has been discussed as logical impossibility. No one can believe a statement which involves a direct contradiction, but short of that, there is no final rule that can be laid down as to what is credible always and everywhere alike. The standard shifts from age to age, from place to place, from one level of intelligence to another, and from one stage of experience to another.

Thus it is not at all difficult to find examples of what are to-day unquestioned and unquestionable facts which even within the last hundred years were contemptuously dismissed as mere legends or mere superstitions, and regarded as quite incredible. The process is always the same. The strange fact is denied outright because there is no explanation of it ready to hand in contemporary science. Then when some discovery is made which allows us to understand the cause of it in some measure, and so to fit it into our scientific scheme, the fact is at last admitted. Thus there existed from time immemorial a widespread belief among the peasantry in many lands that seed should be sown during the period of the moon's increase, because then it grew faster. This was described by a responsible writer, about 1828, as a superstition, " which is now completely exploded, except in some remote and unenlightened districts ".[3] A couple of generations later, about 1870, another writer (who was an eminent authority on folk-lore) described the belief as a survival of " astrological doctrine " and regarded it as quite baseless.[4]

But the belief is well warranted, as recent science has proved. It was discovered by Dr. Semmens, of the University of Liverpool, that the germination of some seeds is materially accelerated by moonlight, the reason being the enhancement of hydrolysis of the reserve food material. This effect was later shown to be due to polarized light. During the daytime photosynthesis takes place in the formation of temporary starch which is deposited within the tissue. During the night this starch disappears, being hydrolized to simpler substances which are soluble, and form the food of the growing plant. This hydrolysis is caused by the polarized light from the moon in its early phases. The quantitative observations of Knauthe showed, in the case of the photosynthetic plankton in the Mississippi basin, that moonlight is more than one hundred thousand times as effective as sunlight in this respect. The widespread belief of simple folk, based, of course, on long observation and experience, but contemptuously dismissed years ago as an incredible superstition, is therefore fully justified by modern science.

To give a second example of a very different kind, another responsible writer, in 1847, poured scorn on the account of the *stigmata* in the life of St. Francis of Assisi as " a legend which would have been rejected as extravagant by the authors to whom we owe the *Arabian Nights* ".[5] Yet probably every sane man to-day who has looked into the evidence will

[3] Whateley, *Elements of Rhetoric*, p. 57.
[4] Sir Edward B. Tylor, *Primitive Culture*, I, p. 130.
[5] Article on " Saint Francis of Assisi " in the *Edinburgh Review*, July 1847.

admit that the marks were really there on the saint's body, and that the same strange phenomenon has happened in the lives of other saints. First of all the fact is contemptuously denied, because it has a look of the miraculous. Then when a good deal of research has been done in morbid psychology and many examples of such strange markings have been recorded and studied, it is gradually admitted that the "extravagant legend" is a fact.

Then it is obvious that the general credibility of any alleged fact not only appears to vary with the degree of what may be called scientific prejudice, based upon the present condition of research, but does quite genuinely vary with the amount and the quality of the evidence, and with the ability and the character of the witnesses. We might well hesitate to believe some strange narrative if it came from a single person of low intelligence, when it would be quite a different matter if it were attested by a number of educated people. Again we might doubt the fact if the story were one the narrators of which were men of poor character, who stood to gain largely by what they told us, whereas our doubts would be greatly diminished if those who told the tale were men of the highest probity, and absolutely disinterested. Innumerable details like these modify our readiness to believe or otherwise in what at first seems unlikely to be true. The most important of these conditioning factors are probably determined by what may be called the range of experience both in the percipient and in the age in which he lives.

The extreme difficulty of defining the incredible beyond any reasonable challenge is well illustrated in one of T. H. Huxley's writings. There is a well-known passage in his study of Hume in which he writes, "If a man tells me that he saw a piebald horse in Piccadilly, I believe him without hesitation. The thing itself is likely enough, and there is no imaginable motive for his deceiving me. But if the same person tells me he observed a zebra there, I might hesitate a little about accepting his testimony unless I were well satisfied, not only as to his previous acquaintance with zebras, but as to his powers and opportunities of observation in the present case. If, however, my informant assured me that he beheld a centaur trotting down that famous thoroughfare, I should emphatically decline to credit his statement: and this even if he were the most saintly of men and ready to suffer martyrdom in support of his belief."[6] Now I do not know that anyone who is concerned to defend the supernatural need object to Huxley's conclusion here, but a double objection to the whole paragraph must be advanced; first, as to the assumption that underlies it all, which is an entirely misleading one, and, second, as to the unfair selection of examples that look more or less parallel, but are really nothing of the sort.

First, then, Huxley did not realize that he was setting up a standard of credibility which only applies in one part of it to a modern Englishman, and his experience of particular facts, under the conditions of the eighteen-nineties. The presumption is that here is an illustration of the general principle of credibility, but in fact that principle is neither permanent nor universal. It is not applicable to all men, all ages, and all events. Thus it is true that there was nothing unlikely in seeing a piebald horse in Piccadilly in 1894, but it never occurred to Huxley (and, of course, could not occur to him) that this very ordinary phenomenon in his own lifetime would be almost a portent to-day, and that it may well be incredible and all but impossible in 1994. The probability of it has immensely decreased with the prevalence of the motor and will most likely decrease to zero in the future. Similarly changed degrees of probability and of improbability may be easily imagined as to Huxley's second example—though it should be observed here, with regard to illustrations such as the next, that if the imaginary example looks rather fantastic, it is merely because it has not yet occurred in our experience: if it did occur it would at once begin to look ordinary. Let us suppose that zebras became extremely valuable for their pelts, and were bred extensively on zebra farms near London (as has happened, for example, with silver foxes in several parts of England and the United States): then it would no longer be a very unlikely thing

[6] *Collected Essays*, VI, p. 158.

to see a zebra, or a herd of zebras, passing down a street in London.

Then, in the second place, Huxley's last example of the centaur is something very like a dishonest trick of argument. There seems at first sight to be a fair parallel between a horse, a zebra, and a centaur, because a zebra is a horse-like creature, and a centaur is also a horse-like creature. But there is no real parallel at all, because we know that two of the creatures are real and that the other is unreal. Horses and zebras do exist, and their existence is familiar to men, for everyone has seen a horse, and everyone has seen at least a picture of a zebra, and knows that this animal exists in some parts of the world. Whereas everyone knows on the other hand that the centaur is fabulous, and no question of credibility really arises with regard to it. The supposed appearance of the horse and the zebra in Piccadilly represent what in different degrees and at different periods is more or less credible, because it is more or less probable. The centaur represents what is quite incredible, because it is quite impossible in the actual state of nature. In other words, Huxley simply *assumes* that a miracle is incredible: then selects an obvious example of the incredible; contrasts this with two examples of what is more or less credible; and then says, " There you are! a miracle is incredible "—which is simply the assumption with which he began.

There is not, as a mere matter of fact, any permanent and universal standard of what is credible and incredible, with the exception, as has been said before, of logical impossibilities. It is perfectly obvious, if you think for a moment, that events which are credible in one place, and in one age, and under one set of conditions, are quite incredible at another place, at another time, and under another set of conditions. What is incredible in tropical Africa to an ignorant savage, is perfectly credible to a civilized man in a northern land, as when the missionary, to interest the natives who were travelling with him, told them that in his native land, at one season of the year, the water in the rivers became solid, so that one could walk across, and even drive a wagon across. To those natives who had never seen ice that was an incredible story, and they rolled on the ground in ecstasies of mirth, because they thought it the most amazing lie they had ever heard.

Similarly, some things which would have been absolutely incredible when I was a child, because they had never happened in human experience then, are credible enough to-day, because we know that they do happen now. Television, for example, which in my childhood could never have been even imagined, except as a fairy-tale about a witch's magic mirror, is a fairly familiar fact in our day.

There is, in fact, no fixed ratio of credibility, and there cannot be. Many things that would be incredible if attributed to ordinary persons in ordinary circumstances may be credible enough when they are ascribed to unusual persons in a special environment, and still more credible when associated with a unique person who lived and acted under unique conditions—if such a person ever existed. It is significant that men have never associated the miraculous with ordinary persons or ordinary experiences: it is some person of extraordinary saintliness who is credited with miracles, or it is in some period when religious experience has reached an extraordinary intensity that miracles are said to have occurred. It may be argued, of course, that such persons and such periods induce a special state of credulity, but it is much more likely that they constitute the spiritual conditions under which the miraculous occurs. I am sure it is not too much to say that anyone who has experienced a religious revival of the genuine kind among Methodists will be prepared to credit many extraordinary events, and some things that are on the verge of physical miracle, if they are not beyond that verge.

The plain fact is that there is not, and there cannot be, any absolute standard of credibility, any more than of possibility, apart from such suppositions as are mere contradictions in terms. The mind instinctively rejects such suppositions as incredible, because they are impossible; as no sane man would hesitate for a moment to reject the statement that two is equal to four. Apart from such incredibilities as this—suppositions which are absolutely incredible because they are absolutely impossible—there is nothing absolutely incredible. Everything else is relatively credible or incredible—relatively to the evidence, the person who makes the statement, the time and the place of the supposed event, the conditions under which it is said to have occurred, and a thousand other circumstances which make it—in that particular complex of relations—more or less credible. A miracle, or a strange providence, or a wonderful answer to prayer, is not inherently either impossible or incredible, and no one has any conceivable right, on any logical grounds, to say that it is.

II

THE NATURAL AND THE SUPERNATURAL

II

THE NATURAL AND THE SUPERNATURAL

WHAT do we really mean by the antithesis between the natural and the supernatural? It is obvious that these terms are correlatives: it is only when you have the conception of the natural to start with that you can have any conception of the supernatural. You must have some notion of the extent and the character of what you call nature and the natural before there is any meaning in speaking of the supernatural, or what is beyond nature. Now the main meaning that we attach to the concept of nature in modern times is that it is the realm of natural law—the region where things happen regularly and repeatedly and in accordance with what we call the laws of nature. The stress is here upon the ordered regularity of nature: the existence of regular causation and the operation of regular laws is assumed everywhere in the universe, and all arbitrariness is excluded. That would be a fair description of what is called the scientific view of the universe. Let it be said quite plainly here that in these pages this view is frankly and fully accepted. This conception of the world as the realm of natural law is often described loosely as if it were the creation of science within the last century or so, yet it was never more exactly expressed, perhaps, than in the words of one who was not a nineteenth-century scientist but a seventeenth-century philosopher. Spinoza laid down the principle that " nothing which takes place in nature can be contrary to the universal laws of nature ".[1] That must be true if we understand by nature the whole of organized existence. The definition here is important, because one is constantly meeting with a confused and contradictory conception of nature, even in responsible writers. Nature is dignified with a capital letter, and almost deified in popular thought, but

[1] *Tractatus Theologico-Politicus VI.*

sometimes Nature is taken to mean the system of physical events that is known to us; sometimes the larger system of events, physical and otherwise, that is known to us ; and sometimes the entire system of events of every kind in the universe, whether known to us or not. Now it is undeniable that things may happen, and do happen, that may seem contrary to what we actually know at present of the laws of nature, but it is equally undeniable that nothing can possibly happen that is really contrary to the universal laws of nature.[2] Spinoza's principle must be true if we mean by nature the entire system of actual and possible existence, for it is axiomatic that nothing can take place within that order except according to that order; it is the totality of order, for it is the totality of existence, on the created plane. Nothing can happen, because nothing can exist, outside that universal order. There *is* nothing beyond it, except the First Cause; and even that exception needs to be qualified, for the First Cause must exist within as well as beyond the whole of nature, as it were; or rather, to express it more satisfactorily, the whole of nature, as the totality of created existence, must exist within the First Cause, as the creative principle. It seems to be still necessary, by the way, in speaking of the First Cause, to guard against the vulgar error of taking the phrase to mean merely a prior cause—the cause that comes first in time, so to speak.[3] Time is succession, and can only

[2] Dr. Tennant states that " science leaves theology free to assert the possibility of miracle, but seems to preclude the possibility of our being able to pronounce a marvel to be a miracle in the objective or absolute sense of the word: the sense, i.e. in which it denotes incapability for all time of being subsumed under natural law ". (*Miracle and its Philosophical Presuppositions*, pp. 32-33.) What does " natural law " mean here? If it means the system of law which rules the whole of existence, then anything which can never be brought under that system is not only impossible, it is inconceivable. Such a definition of miracle at once makes it literally unthinkable. If " natural law " here means the laws of nature *as known to men at any given period* then it is obvious that there is always the possibility of events which transcend our knowledge of any such laws at any such period. Indeed, all scientific discovery is an illustration of the fact.

[3] " For the first cause is not, of course, as is sometimes absurdly supposed, the earliest of an infinite series of antecedents . . . but a power which differs in kind from all its effects, and is not only, to speak in temporal language,

come into existence with the universe, and the First Cause does not mean a cause that was first in order of succession : it means the *causa causarum*, the Cause of all causes, the original and originating ground of all reality, which is as necessary to explain the continued existence of all things as to explain the origin of their existence at the first.[4]

Now if we say that the totality of created existence must exist within the First Cause as the creative principle, that is only to say that the Universal and Absolute Cause must be conceived as existing in a universal and absolute way. Every particular existence is partial, relative and dependent; it is a fragment of existence, and is interrelated with the whole of dependent existence. But God, as the uncaused Cause of all, is before all, within all, beyond all, and the whole of created existence exists, as it were, within the sphere of His uncreated and creative Being, and depends not only for its origin, but for its continuance, upon His causal

the past creator, but also the present sustainer of that continuous process of events which constitutes the life of the world. And when, for intellectual convenience, we separate any antecedent and consequent parts of this process into causes and effects, we are only using the term " cause " in a secondary sense, which must not be confused with the fact of primary causation. The former only transmits, while the latter originates energy."—Illingworth, *Divine Transcendence*, p. 26.

[4] Die Erhaltung (*conservatio*) ist diejenige göttliche Thätigkeit, vermöge welcher Gott alle seine Geschöpfe in ihrer ursprünglichen Wesenheit in der Zeit fortdauern lässt. Ohne diese göttliche Erhaltung würde die Welt sofort wieder in das Nichts zürucksinken ; denn die geschaffenen Dinge haben nicht in sich selbst die Kraft ihrer Subsistenz, auch nicht einer zeitweiligen. . . . Die Erhaltung ist eine fortwährende Einwirkung (*Influxus*) Gottes auf die Welt mittelst seiner Wesensallgegenwart (*omnipraesentia substantialis*). Sie steht übrigens im engsten Zusammenhange mit der Schöpfung ; in Gott sind beide Ein und derselbe Act, und nur wir unterscheiden beide. Deshalb nennen die altkirchlichen Dogmatiker nach dem Vorgange der Scholastiker die Erhaltung eine fortdauernde Schöpfung.—Rothe, *Dogmatik*, I, pp. 161-162.

(" Conservation is that divine activity by virtue of which God maintains the whole of His creation in time in its original reality. Without this divine conservation the world would at once fall back into nothingness; for created things have no power of self-subsistence, not even temporarily. . . . This conservation is a continuous influence of God upon the world by means of His omnipresence. Moreover, it stands in the closest relation to the act of creation: in God both are one and the same act, and they are only distinguished in our thought. Therefore the older theologians of the Church, following the Schoolmen, describe the conservation as a continuous creation.")

activity. The finite exists within the infinite, and depends for its existence upon the infinite. But if the point is safeguarded that God cannot be merely included in the universe (which is only saying that the absolute cannot be included in the relative, and the infinite in the finite) it must remain true that everything that happens, or that can happen, in nature must happen according to the universal laws of nature. There cannot possibly be any quarrel between science and religion on that point—if the scientist and the theologian really understand the issue. Any exception to the regularity of natural law can only be an apparent exception, which appears to be such because of the limited knowledge and the limited experience of the observer. A scientist, confronted by an apparent breach of natural laws as they are known to him, could never conclude that this was some causeless, lawless, unrelated fact, standing outside the whole of the ordered existence of the universe: such a thing will be found to be strictly inconceivable if you try to think out what it means. The scientist would at once conclude that here was a hitherto unobserved fact which *must* fit in somehow into the ordered scheme of nature, though he might have to confess that he did not know in the least what the cause and the law which governed the fact might be. These he would then set himself to discover, in perfect confidence that they existed, and might some day be found out.

This, which is unquestionable as regards any fact from the scientific point of view, is equally unquestionable from a religious point of view. Nothing could conceivably be a breach of law in the sight of God, for omniscience would see all things in a perfect and ultimate order: every fact that seems to our limited knowledge an exception, an anomaly, a portent, must in the infinite knowledge of God fall into its ordered place in the universal scheme. Thus it is true to say that nothing would be a miracle to God. There could be no natural or supernatural for an infinite intelligence, for all that we call natural and supernatural would be comprehended in one universal order of existence. There may be a real exception to a partial order, or an apparent exception to the universal order as partially known, but there could not conceivably be a real exception to the universal order when that order is thought of as completely known. Such a thing would be absolutely isolated, absolutely arbitrary, having no cause, obeying no law, existing without any relation to anything else, standing outside the whole universe, a thing which (while we are trying to suppose it real) is yet by definition beyond the whole of reality. Such a thing is unthinkable.

The theologian, when confronted with a miracle in which he believes, no more attempts to suppose such an inconceivable account of it than the scientist would, when confronted with some inexplicable fact. Like the scientist he says: Here is a hitherto unaccountable fact which *must* fit in somehow into the universal order: it must have some cause and it must obey some law. But he does not forget, as the scientist sometimes does, that we do not yet understand all the causes and laws that are at work in the universe, and he does not conclude, as the scientist sometimes does, that the miracle must be explicable entirely in the terms of normal physics, or else be denied as an impossibility. He refers the miracle to the operation of a higher cause and a higher law, which are not yet understood by our limited human intelligence.[5] He is quite willing to believe that some day we may

[5] Dr. Tennant has observed, in commenting upon Mozley, that a reference to " higher laws " in regard to miracle is useless to the apologist, because " the outcome would be that for any alleged miracle a natural explanation might in time be forthcoming. That would involve surrender of the evidential value of miracle, the one function which was then generally deemed essential to miracle." (*Miracle and its Philosophical Presuppositions*, p. 28.) I do not think a phrase like " the evidential value of miracle " can properly be used of the attitude of the older apologists to the supernatural without a good deal of explanation and qualification. But, apart from that, how does the fact that a natural explanation might *later* be forthcoming affect the present quality of a miracle? even the evidential quality of it? It does not affect it at all. One of our Lord's miracles would still be a miracle as wrought by Him two thousand years ago, even if two thousand years hence men could achieve the same result by what to them were natural means. A little later Dr. Tennant says that " the arbitrary supposition that there are such higher laws is irrelevant to the problem as long as the criterion of miracle is taken to be incompatibility with such law as we do know. The resolution of natural abnormalities into higher normalities, is beside the question " (p. 29). I do not believe that it

be able to understand the cause and the law which govern the miracle: whether in some future age by the progress of scientific discovery, or in a higher world, when we know even as we are known. Here or hereafter we shall learn to see the miracle as a consistent, and, so to speak, regular detail in the whole of the ordered regularity of the universe.[6]

Many, if not most, of the fallacies that beset modern thought about the supernatural are due, as we have already suggested, to the ambiguous use of the term Nature. The word is often used as if it were equivalent to the universe, or the totality of existence: and there is no particular objection to such a use of the word *if we remember that this is what we mean.* But we sometimes forget that this meaning includes all that exists, whether it is known to us or not, and then go on to use the word Nature in a different sense, meaning the range of existing facts as familiarly known and experienced by humanity. Now it is only in regard to this second sense of the word nature that the word supernatural can have any meaning at all. There cannot be anything beyond the whole range of existence; there can only be that which is beyond the range of existence as far as it is known to us and experienced by us.[7] It is the distinction made by St.

is, for a moment. What could be an " abnormality " to God, or to some superhuman intelligence which, seeing all at once, would necessarily see all things in the universe as linked into one complete and therefore " normal " order? The criterion of miracle is incompatibility with such law as we know, only in the sense that miracle is unexplained as yet by such law as we know. The example of the Röntgen ray, which Dr. Tennant himself alleges, will serve as an illustration. For men to be able to see by means of these rays what they had not been able to see before was incompatible with the natural laws that men had known up to then, not in the sense that it really contradicted or cancelled these laws, though it might appear to do so, but in the sense that it was not explicable by these laws, and was only to be explained by other laws hitherto unknown, which is what Mozley means by " higher laws".

[6] Butler, *Analogy of Religion,* I. i, p. 33.

[7] This is the view of Locke. In the *Essay on the Human Understanding* (XVI, 13) he writes of " supernatural events . . . which may be the fitter to procure belief, by how much the more they are beyond or contrary to ordinary observation. This is the proper case of miracles." And in the *Essay on Miracle* he defines a miracle as " a sensible operation which, being above the comprehension of the spectator, and in his opinion contrary to the established course of Nature, is taken by him to be divine ".

Augustine long ago, when he said that a miracle is *non contra naturam, sed contra quam est nota natura.*[8] That distinction is an inevitable and irrefragable one. Nature, meaning the absolute sum of all existence, is one concept : nature, meaning existence so far as it is known to us, is quite another. The whole process of scientific progress illustrates this, for it is the gradual enlargement of our knowledge of nature. A scientific discovery does not create a new law or a new force: it only finds out a law or a force which has been operating in the universe ever since the universe began, but which had been unknown to man up to that point. Since no one will be foolish enough to think that we know everything about the universe yet, there must be many more laws and forces that are still unknown, but that will one day be discovered. Now the supernatural, in this sense, *must* exist, and *does* exist, for there is unquestionably a range of facts, forces, and laws as yet unknown to us—otherwise there would be nothing left for science to discover. This is absolutely the only meaning that can intelligently be given to the supernatural. It cannot

[8] Omnia quippe portenta contra naturam dicimus esse; sed non sunt. Quo modo est enim contra naturam, quod Dei fit voluntate, cum voluntas tanti utique conditoris conditae rei cuius que natura sit? Portentum ergo fit non contra naturam, sed contra quam est nota natura. *De civ. Dei*, XXI, 8.

(" For we say that all portents are contrary to nature, but they are not so. For how is that contrary to nature which happens by the will of God, since the will of so mighty a Creator is certainly the nature of each created thing? A portent, therefore, happens not contrary to nature, but contrary to what we know as nature.")

Compare the following passage :

Sed contra naturam non incongrue dicimus aliquid Deum facere, quod facit contra id quod novimus in natura. Hanc enim etiam appellamus naturam, cognitum nobis cursum solitumque naturae, contra quem Deus cum aliquid facit, magnalia vel mirabilia nominantur. Contra illam vero summam naturae legem, a notitia remotam, sive impiorum, sive adhuc infirmorum, tam Deus nullo modo facit, quam contra seipsum non facit. *Contra Faustum*, XXVI, 3.

(" There is, however, no impropriety in saying that God does a thing contrary to nature, when it is contrary to what we know of nature. For we give the name nature to the usual common course of nature; and whatever God does contrary to this, we call a prodigy, or a miracle. But against the supreme law of nature, which is beyond the knowledge both of the ungodly and of weak believers, God never acts, any more than He acts against Himself.")

be anything beyond nature in the wider sense, that is to say, beyond the universe. That would be a contradiction in terms. It would mean that when you have included absolutely everything that exists in a final total of reality, there is still something else left over, which is absurd. Nothing can conceivably exist that is not within nature, in the sense of being within the universe. But many things exist in the universe that were not within the experience of men in the past, and many things exist in the universe that are not yet within our experience to-day. Some of these things were once beyond nature, as far as men knew nature then, and some are now beyond nature, as far as men know nature to-day.

The supernatural, then, in the only sense in which the word can have any warrantable meaning, is relative to human experience.[9] The wireless would be supernatural, in the strictest sense of the word, to a savage. It would be something entirely beyond his experience, and entirely beyond his understanding—a fact that he had never encountered before, and that he could not explain when he did encounter it. I do not say that it would *seem to be* a miracle to him ; I say that it would *be* a miracle to him, in the most rigid meaning of the word. It illustrates what has been said before to point out that, in this example of the savage and the wireless, there is no new element of reality, so to speak, involved in the thing that is strange to him, but only a new

[9] Dr. Tennant demurs to the statement that "no line of demarcation between the natural and the supernatural admits of being drawn" (p. 38). But it seems quite obvious that you can only draw such a line, in the sense which he means, if you know the limits of the natural, which it is quite certain that nobody in the world does, or can do. Our knowledge of the natural widens every day. There are facts and factors in the natural universe that were totally unknown when I was a boy. There must be a vast multitude of facts and factors in the natural universe that are still unknown. How can you say, in the absolute sense, "Here the supernatural begins," when you do not know where the natural ends? How can you say what is beyond nature when you do not know, and cannot know, where the frontier of nature lies? You can say that the limit of ordinary human experience or ordinary human knowledge lies here or hereabout, but that is all that you can possibly say. In other words the line of demarcation between the natural and the supernatural lies not at the unknown and unknowable limit of nature, but at the limit of nature as known by men, as experienced by men, at any given period.

control, and a new use, due to a new understanding, of real elements in the universe that have always been present in the world, and that have always been known, in a rudimentary way, to the savage. He knows sound, and he knows lightning, but has no scientific knowledge of acoustics or electricity, and so he does not know how to use electricity to transmit and reproduce sound. The miracle to the savage —and it would be strictly a miracle to him—does not lie in a fact which is strange to all men and inexplicable to all men. It lies in a fact which is strange to *his* experience and inexplicable to *his* mind. If the savage becomes civilized, and educated, and learns some science, and begins to understand the nature of sound and of electricity, and the structure of a wireless set, the thing is no more a miracle to him. It is really as wonderful a thing as ever it was, but as he becomes familiar with the fact, and finds that the explanation of it falls into line with the rest of our knowledge, the wonder fades, and the thing that was supernatural to him, when it was strange and unexplained, becomes natural to him, now that it is familiar and explained.

These two elements of familiarity and of understanding are closely allied, and for this reason: when we are thoroughly familiar with an event, because it is one that constantly recurs, it seems to fall into place in the regular system of our experience, and therefore we conclude, quite rightly, that it must fall into place in a regular system of external existence. That is mainly what we mean by "understanding" anything. In the ultimate sense we do not understand anything at all. Why anything should exist, and why everything should exist as it does, we do not know, and we can only reach the last frontier of enquiry either by simply confessing final ignorance, or by referring everything to the inscrutable will of God. It is the barest truth to say that, in the last resort, either all we know ends in what we do not know, and what is unknowable to any mind, which is an attitude of intellectual despair; or that all that we know and do not know ends in the infinite knowledge of God, which is an attitude of faith. But in any case we cannot know " the reason of the cause and the wherefore of the why ", because our knowledge is limited, and the finality of truth is limitless. An absolutely complete knowledge of anything that exists would mean an absolutely complete knowledge of everything that exists, for all things in the universe are interrelated and interdependent. That absolute knowledge is plainly impossible to the limited mind of man. If it exists anywhere it exists alone in the mind of God.

But while our knowledge of the universe is very far from complete, it is progressive. The mind of man is always extending the area of its researches, and we are able to explore additional regions of knowledge one by one and bring them into ordered relation to the realm of existing knowledge. The progress of human knowledge is like the process of filling in a crossword puzzle. Here is a blank which baffles you, and you cannot imagine what the right word may be. Presently you get one or two letters of other words as cross-clues, and the right word suggests itself. You are more or less sure that it is the right word, because it fits in better than any other with the whole arrangement of words, and to that extent helps to make an ordered and intelligible whole. This particular word does not explain its own existence, or the existence of the other words, or the existence of the whole puzzle—except in so far as it falls into place in what is plainly a planned and purposeful scheme, which therefore implies that it is the work of intelligence. So it is with any sort of scientific theory. It justifies itself by the way that it tallies accurately with the rest of our knowledge: it really explains nothing, either as to the existence of the particular range of facts to which it relates, or as to the existence of the whole of nature, except as it brings these facts into an orderly and intelligible relation to all the other facts we know, and therefore suggests that the whole universe is orderly, and the creation of intelligence.

So that, while our knowledge of the universe is incomplete, it is consistent, as far as it goes. It is ordered knowledge of an ordered world, and there could be no knowledge of a world that was altogether disorderly; indeed, such a world is wholly inconceivable. As a matter of fact every man believes this to be an orderly and ordered world, that is to say, a planned and purposeful world. That presupposition is necessary not only to all thought, but to all action. We could not live at all unless this were true in fact, and also taken for granted in all our thoughts and deeds. Imagine an entirely erratic universe—if you can. Think of a world where you might wake up to-morrow morning to find that it was the week before last; or that the law of gravitation had been unaccountably reversed, so that everything that was not fastened down was rising into the air; or that the sun had suddenly increased in bulk a thousandfold, or diminished to the size of the moon—in which case, of course, no human being would exist very long to witness the fact. But even wild illustrations like these miss the mark, for if such amazing changes came to pass, the mind of man, if man still existed, would instantly set to work to speculate on the reason and the cause of such phenomena. It would always be assumed by the human intellect that there *was* a reason and a cause: in other words, that the universe, however strangely it might be behaving, was still somehow a rational and purposive scheme.

As a matter of fact we cannot conceive an orderless, purposeless, irrational world. If we try to imagine a mere chaos, for example, we cannot help thinking of it as a whole, and therefore a unity, and as a whole that exists within the conceptual framework of space and time, and as a whole in which there is some internal relation between every part, at least a relation of likeness and unlikeness. That means that it is *not* a mere chaos: it may be a chaos relatively to the cosmos we know, but it is not sheer causelessness, sheer unrelatedness, sheer unaccountableness. That cannot be imagined. It may be *stated*, as a kind of negation—the absence of the causation and relation and rationality to which we are accustomed in this universe, but it cannot be *thought*. It is impossible to represent it to the mind as a fact.

Surely that is suggestive. It means that we cannot think at all without assuming that there is some sort of order, and arrangement, and therefore purpose, in the universe. It may well be beyond the power of the human mind to discern that purpose in all its extent, but we cannot think of the universe in which we dwell without taking it for granted that it is purposive and therefore rational.

Now whenever we speak of reason and purpose we imply a personal existence and a personal activity. An impersonal reason and an impersonal purpose are quite inconceivable. To speak of reason and purpose unless we mean the reason and purpose that is ultimately that of a person is to use words without meaning. We know absolutely nothing of these things except as the attributes of personality, and we have no real right to recognize them in the world (as all men do, in spite of themselves) unless we proceed to the inevitable conclusion that the order, purpose, and intelligence which are exhibited everywhere in the universe, and which come to consciousness in man, are the signature of God. But if God exists and rules there can be nothing to forbid the belief that He brings to pass events which are so strange that we call them supernatural, and that these are seen not only in miracles, but in the way that our lives are guided, and our prayers answered, when we put our trust in Him.

III

CAUSATION

III

CAUSATION

IT is rather surprising to find how much of the difficulty felt by many minds in conceiving of any real action of God in the natural world arises from a fallacious idea of the nature of causation. It often seems to be thought that a cause and an effect follow each other, so to speak, in single file—as if every particular cause and every particular effect were a separate entity, and as if these followed each other in a predestined line of necessary succession. Then, when it is a matter of miracle, or providential guidance, or answered prayer, the question arises, Is it to be supposed that one of these causes can be somehow irregularly taken out of the line of succession, and another somehow irregularly substituted for it ?—thus disturbing what is regarded as an inevitable series of sequences.

But an event is not brought to pass by a single cause : it is brought about by a multiplicity of causes acting together in a very complex way. The picture needed in our minds is not something like a string of beads, but something like a game of chess. The pattern of causation is not linear, but reticular: it is not a straight line in which one effect follows from one cause in a single series which is fixed, but an involved network in which an effect follows from a multitude of causes, in a multiplex series which is continually changing. Both these points are extremely important.

First, then, it is not strictly true to say that any event has *a* cause ; it has a multitude of causes. We say that the cause of a man's death is a bullet through the head, and that serves well enough as a rough and ready statement of fact. But it is very defective if we want a complete account of what has happened. We have merely picked out one prominent detail in the complex of causation, and have either deliberately ignored all the other causal factors, or, if we are rather elementary thinkers, we have perhaps entirely forgotten them for the moment. An adequate statement of the cause of the man's death would have to include not only the bullet, but the explosive mixture which impelled the bullet; and the form of the gun, which restricted and directed the force of the explosion; and the exact aim of the weapon, since if it had been pointed otherwise the bullet would have missed the man; and the position of the gun in space, since if it had been ten miles off the man would not have been hit; and the moment of the explosion in time, since if it had happened a hundred years ago the dead man would not then have been born; and the existence of chemical substances such as sulphur and saltpetre and charcoal and nitroglycerine, since without these there would have been no explosive, and ultimately the entire physical constitution and history of the universe, because if the evolution of the solar system and the geological history of the earth had been different these chemical substances with their properties might never have existed at all.

Moreover, the man would not have died by the bullet unless the human organism had been such that severe laceration of the brain is a fatal injury; and there are many other factors, such as the man's position in space and time at the moment when the gun was fired, since if he had been somewhere else in the world, or if it had been another hour or another day, the bullet would not have reached him; and the man's height, since if he had been six inches shorter the bullet would have missed his head; and the early physical life of the man, and indeed his whole complex ancestry, since his stature results from the conditions of his early nurture and of his ancestral history; and finally the whole evolution of organic life upon this planet, since apart from that humanity would never have existed at all, and there would have been no man to be shot. The cause of the man's death, therefore, is not merely the bullet, but an immense, complex, and prolonged series of facts and factors which finally include everything in the universe, past and present.

In point of fact the whole notion of causation is derived

from our own experience, and, as it were, imposed upon the world of nature: our only actual experience of it is in our own personal relation to the external world. When once man has arrived at the conception he finds that it is a necessity of thought, for all things hang together, and nothing happens of itself and by itself. To speak of cause and effect is simply a recognition of that fact—that all things in the universe are interconnected and interdependent. We find that it is always necessary, as a great philosopher has said, " to connect changes with conditions ",[1] and, as we carry out that process we find that it is necessary to connect every single change with all the multiple conditions; in other words that everything that happens in the world is really the result of everything else that happens, or has happened.

There can be no question that this, however paradoxical it may seem at first sight, is simply a statement of fact. And it has an important bearing on the nature and the range of human knowledge. As the complete cause of anything really involves the action of everything else in the universe, so a complete account of anything would really involve a knowledge of everything else in the universe. Here, for example, is my pocket-knife. It exists; it exists in space and in time; it is constructed of steel and bone, which are special forms of matter; and it is moved by my hand when in use. A complete knowledge of the pocket-knife would therefore mean a complete knowledge of the nature of existence, of space, of time, of matter and of motion—in other words a complete knowledge of the nature of the physical universe. Even that is not all, for the knife is a product of human intelligence, and in use is an instrument of human volition, so that we should have to add to what is needed for a complete knowledge of it a complete knowledge of the nature of intelligence and of volition and of the relation of the human

[1] " On the whole, the ordinary notion of Cause and Effect is but a clumsy expression of the necessary law which requires us to connect changes with conditions, and is plainly enough derived from experience of our own activity, and the contrast of the living nature that acts and the lifeless thing that suffers."—Lotze, *Microcosmos,* I, p. 677.

mind and the human will to all the other facts of existence. And so of everything else: an absolutely complete knowledge of anything that exists in the universe would mean a final understanding of the universe itself.[2] The poet is expressing an elementary truth of philosophy—which after all is only what any intelligent man must see if he thinks for five minutes—when he writes:

> "Flower in the crannied wall,
> I pluck you out of the crannies,
> I hold you here, root and all, in my hand,
> Little flower—but *if* I could understand
> What you are, root and all, and all in all,
> I should know what God and man is."

Then, in the second place, not only has every event a multitude of causes, but the precise arrangement of those causes is itself a causal factor, and that arrangement is constantly changing, so that a measureless variety of events may come to pass by the continual rearrangement of all the causes that are at work in the world. That, again, is an unquestionable fact. The causes are actually regrouped from moment to moment, so that the effects which result from them are changed from moment to moment, and an almost infinite variety of happenings come to pass in consequence. It is quite obvious that the very same causes, reassembled into another order, will produce different results. When you add up the figures in the cash columns of a ledger the total is not determined merely by the presence of all the figures but also by their position. Let a figure be changed from one column to another and the total will differ. The figure is still there, and is still an item in the total, but the change of position has given it a different value, and therefore the total is different. Without putting in any figure that is not there, or taking away any figure that is there, a rearrangement of the figures will give a different result, and if there are a great many figures involved, the possible rearrangements of them will give thousands of different results. So it is, and so

[2] Cf. A. E. Taylor, *Elements of Metaphysics*, p. 35.

it must be, with the causes which operate in the world. The actual causes may be precisely the same, but a shifting of the order and the relation of the causes will give another result and a very different one.

Take the weather as an example. It is the result of a vast number of different factors—the amount of heat from the sun and of evaporation from the sea, the direction and force of many currents in the ocean and in the air, the neighbourhood of mountains and forests, the distance of any particular district from a torrid desert or from a snowy steppe or from the sea, the amount of sunshine or of rain in preceding months and so on. Some of these factors are more or less permanent; some of them are exceedingly variable; but it is the entire grouping of all these that determines the weather. That actual grouping of permanent and changeable factors does alter from day to day, from hour to hour, and so the weather alters. It is therefore not merely this, that, or the other factor that determine what the weather will be, nor merely all of them together, but the way that they are all grouped in relation to each other. In other words, it is not any single cause, nor even the mere totality of causes, but the precise arrangement of all the causes that brings about a particular effect.[3]

This is a point of very great importance, and it is constantly forgotten in arguments that deal with the possibility and the probability of events. The world is, as a matter of fact, a kaleidoscope of constantly changing events, and this means that there is a constantly changing interplay of cause and effect. There is a causal scheme behind the range of actual events, and that scheme alters from moment to moment. What governs its perpetual change? There is a particular arrangement at this moment, which will be different at the next moment; what determines the shifting pattern as it constantly changes?

The ultimate issue, then, with regard to any action of God in the world of nature, whether it is what we call miracle, or what we call providential direction, or what we call an

[3] W. McDougall, *Modern Materialism and Emergent Evolution*, pp. 72-73.

answer to prayer, is really this : Is there any direction of the whole sum of events in the universe, or is there not ? Any particular event is brought about by the totality of present and previous causes. Obviously there is a total pattern of facts and factors in the universe at any and every moment, and obviously it changes from moment to moment. What determines that perpetually changing pattern in its infinite intricacy ? What orders, directs, and controls all the combinations of causes in the universe ? There is no real answer to that question except by way of theism. That is certainly not too much to say, if you consider the possible answers to the problem. What are they ? If you rule out a belief in God, the only alternatives are fate and chance, and both these are impossible conceptions, if you really think out what they mean.

The whole question as to any control of causes finally becomes another problem, that of the origin of the universe. No one denies the existence of order in the actual working of the universe from moment to moment. Every scientist, and for that matter, everybody else, takes it for granted that events are actually related to one another, and do actually depend upon one another, in a regular sequence of causation, and to that extent there is a universal order. But is that order purposive, or is it merely automatic ? Our belief as to that depends upon our conception of the origin of existence. What was it that at the beginning established what everyone must admit is the subsequent orderliness of the universe ?

The old-fashioned materialist believed in a kind of fate which originated, apparently, in the nebula. He said that the arrangement of causes in the universe at any moment was determined by the arrangement that existed a moment before that, and so backwards to the beginning.[4] But that seems

[4] " If we ask a man in a new and strange situation why he acts as he does, it will hardly occur to him to explain his conduct by describing to us the immediately preceding situation. The answer he is like to give, and that we naturally expect, will consist rather in describing the end at which he aims and the value that it has for him, as the reason for his determination. But if we ask a physicist to explain an unusual phenomenon he can do so only by discovering its antecedents, tracing these to their antecedents, and so on

literally inconceivable if you try to think out what is involved. The materialist rules out intelligence and purpose and direction at the beginning, and then says, in effect, that all that happens is determined by the nature of primal matter at the beginning of the universe. That means (if indeed it means anything) that all the infinitely complex interactions of all the forces and laws of the universe for millions of years past were ordered from a beginning when there was no order and no source from which order could come—that a causeless disorder contained within itself all the causes and all the order that eventually emerged. It is like saying that a mass of jumbled type on the floor of a printer's shop sorts itself out, sets itself up, and prints itself into a sensible book. It is really even madder than that, for the type has at any rate been designed by intelligence, even if we think of it as left to itself afterward. The universe in its actual being from age to age is a realm of causes, laws, and order, and the whole of science depends upon that fact. But the source of it all, we are told, was a causeless, lawless, orderless chaos of matter, which nevertheless was the matrix of universal destiny. One would think that a really sceptical mind would find it considerably easier to accept the wildest legends of the Middle Ages than to believe in such a cosmogony as that.

The alternative to such a belief in blind fate—though it is not really an alternative, but finally amounts to the very same thing—is a belief in blind chance. It is astonishing that some scientific thinkers who would not dream of bringing such a conception to explain the actual working of the universe from moment to moment, nevertheless attribute the origin of the universe to chance. This is really, in the long run, attributing every single event to chance, though that does not seem to be recognized. But if the origin of the universe is due to chance, the ultimate origin of everything in the universe is due to chance. Now this is an amazing

indefinitely: in other words he can explain it only on the assumption that it is determined by its place in a single rigorous mechanical system."—James Ward, *The Realm of Ends*, pp. 278-9. Compare F. R. Tennant, *Philosophical Theology*, p. 23.

implication for any scientist to accept. Science depends absolutely, as Whitehead has said, upon the belief that " every detailed occurrence can be correlated with its antecedents in a perfectly definite manner, exemplifying general principles "—in other words, that this is a universe where everything happens as the result of the regular operation of cause and effect, in accordance with natural laws. This is fundamental and absolute; it applies to every single fact in the universe. Yet when it comes to the origin of the whole universe itself, from which the whole direction of events in the universe inevitably follows, the principle is deserted, and it is assumed that the cause of all is a sort of unthinkable causelessness, which is then named " chance "—very illogically, since chance cannot conceivably mean that, or anything like that. A very competent writer on science, after quoting Plato to the effect that the whole creation results " from the elements, not by any action of the mind, or of any god, or from art, but by nature and chance only ", goes on to say, " This theory, that everything has come about by chance, through the random action of ' laws of nature ', is probably still the most widely held theory amongst educated people."[5] Consider the astonishing assumptions in this sentence. First, everything has come about by the action of laws of nature, that is to say, the laws of nature are active causes which make things happen. But they are not: they are only abstract statements as to *how* things happen, and have nothing whatever to do with causing them to happen. Second, the action of these laws of nature is random action; but how can any law of nature be random in its action? It cannot act at all, in this sense, but if it could, how could the action of any law be random? Action at random is not regular and related action, such as alone can exist when you are referring to a natural law. Third, everything has come about by chance, as we are told most educated people think.

On this issue, one can only ask, in simple wonder, what " educated people " think they mean by " chance " ? Have they ever asked themselves what the word does mean?

[5] J. W. N. Sullivan, *Limitations of Science*, p. 96.

Chance is a most delusive conception as it is commonly employed,[6] and yet the real meaning of it, the only possible meaning of it, is plain enough if we think for a moment or two. We speak, for example, of games of chance as against games of skill. In the latter a practised ability can bring about a result with more or less certainty, because the forces involved are known, and can be controlled, with more or less accuracy, as the expert billiards player can generally prophesy where the ball will go, because he can generally make it go where he likes. But in a game of chance no practice and no ability will enable us to say exactly what will happen, because the forces at work are less manageable and less calculable. If a pack of cards is thoroughly shuffled, and I am asked to pick one out, I cannot possibly say which card it will turn out to be, because I do not know, and could not remember if I did know, the original order of all the cards, much less see and remember every motion of every card while they are being shuffled, and consequently I do not know what card it is that I am selecting. So when we say that a certain card "chances" to turn up in a game we really mean that we cannot foretell that result, because we do not know, and cannot control, all the conditions that bring about that result. We know that the appearance of that particular card at that particular juncture must be the result of the interplay of natural laws and natural forces, as much as the motion of the billiard ball is, but we cannot measure and manipulate the forces at work in the same way, and thus we cannot in the same way foretell the result. So we say the card "chances" to come uppermost, and we mean by that that we do not know, until it does appear, that it is going to appear. If we could precisely calculate all the forces and combinations and possibilities that are involved in the shuffling of the pack, we know that we *could* prophesy that this particular card would turn up then. But we do not know all these factors ; therefore we cannot prophesy the result, and so we say that it happens by "chance". That means

[6] Cf. Butler, *Analogy of Religion*, II, IV., p. 201, and Lotze, *Microcosmos*, I, p. 677.

merely that we do not know exactly what is going to happen, or exactly how it happens. No sane person thinks that the fact is uncaused: no one can think that. No one supposes for a moment that here is a thing that happens by itself, and of itself, without any relation whatever to anything else in the universe. That is literally and absolutely unthinkable. We know that the thing comes to pass, like everything else in the world, by the normal operation of regular laws and regular forces, but it happens that here we cannot trace all the causes that bring it about, and so cannot anticipate the result.

That is absolutely all that chance can possibly mean, whether we are speaking of a single event in the life of the universe, or whether we are speaking of the origin of the whole universe itself. Therefore to say that all things come about by chance is simply to hypostatize our own ignorance. It is not even to say that the cause of all things is causelessness, which one would think to be a sufficiently absurd and contradictory statement: it is even worse than that. It is to say that it is actually *our ignorance of the cause* that is the cause of all things. We have taken a limitation of our own knowledge, and deified it into the cause of all that is. "Chance", which cannot mean more than "we do not know precisely how the thing comes to pass", is exalted into a cause, and finally into the original and universal cause of all things. Nothing could be more utterly irrational than that. It is reasonable to take the position of a theist, and to say that there is a Universal Cause, which is God. It is reasonable to take the position of an agnostic, and to say that there is a Universal Cause, though we do not know what it may be—which is only saying, in effect, that there is an Unknown God. But it is not in the least rational to say that the Universal Cause is merely our human ignorance of what the cause may be—which is all that can really be signified by the deceptive word "chance". What scientists who speak of the origin of all things as due to "chance" *intend* to mean is, of course, not that the origin of the universe, with all its purpose and direction, is unknown to us, but that there *was* no purpose and no direction at the beginning. But that is very improperly and illogically expressed by the term "chance" which cannot possibly mean anything of the kind, as we have seen. Moreover, the denial of purpose and direction at the beginning is the utter contradiction of what is assumed everywhere except at the beginning. The fundamental principle on which all science is based is that everything has a cause, but what this entirely irrational use of the term chance is meant to suggest is that everything ultimately has no cause, or (to reduce it to a paradox that would make the most paradoxical theologian blush) that mere causelessness is the cause of all that is!

The only rational answer to the final problem is that all the order of the universe is from a Universal Mind which designed it before the beginning, and which directs and effectuates all things continually. Now if that belief in God is admitted there cannot be any scientific difficulty involved with regard to the religious experience of the believer where it connects with natural events, for if all the limitless interactions of natural laws and natural forces are ordered by God then it must be true that He can direct the events of my life, and that He can answer my prayer, if He will, and that He can use unknown laws and forces in the universe (for even the most conceited scientist will not argue that we as yet know all the laws and forces that exist in the universe) to bring about events which are to us strange and supernatural.

IV

THE LAWS OF NATURE

IV

THE LAWS OF NATURE

THERE appears to be much confusion in the minds of many people, and even in the minds of some responsible writers, when they are thinking of the laws of nature, especially in relation to religious faith. That is true alike of nearly all those who attack religion from the angle of physical science, and of many who seek to defend religion from such attacks. Now that confusion is due to some sheer fallacies, which really ought to be quite obvious to anyone who thinks carefully, and these fallacies originate from the use of the word "law" in a quite indefensible sense.[1] Again and again we meet the suggestion, more or less explicit, that events are explained, and even that they are caused, by natural laws. The laws of nature are conceived as if, in their totality, they constitute a causative system which is absolutely rigid and absolutely automatic, so that any direction by God (and the strict logic of it would also involve any direction by man) is either inconceivable, or must be regarded somehow as an external interference with the mechanism, of a very improbable kind.

The fact is, of course, that the conception of law originated in human life, and in respect of human conduct, and the word "law" has been most unhappily transferred to the realm of natural events, where it has carried with it all sorts of illegitimate associations of an anthropomorphic kind. A law in human life means, first of all, a command, and a command which is imposed by some personal authority upon persons. It means also that there is in the command some

[1] "No greater misfortune in my opinion has happened in the history of our vocabulary than that the same word 'law' should be used to designate the command of a sovereign authority and the generalization of a Newton or a Darwin."—Earl of Oxford and Asquith, *Free Thought in the Nineteenth Century*, Essex Hall Lecture, 1925.

Cf. James Ward, *Naturalism and Agnosticism*, p. 541.

moral sanction and some moral appeal which makes the command more or less a matter of right and wrong. It means again that behind the command there is some personal authority which can enforce the command, and make men obey it under penalties. Finally, in consequence of all this it comes to represent a normal standard of human conduct. Thus in our national legislation Parliament issues the command, because it appears to a majority of the representatives of the people the right command to issue. The police and the magistracy enforce the command by punishing those who disobey it. The vast majority of people do obey it in the long run, and so it represents a rule of behaviour.

There are thus at least four distinct elements in the conception of law as we use it in reference to human conduct. It is (*a*) a personal command, which has (*b*) a moral quality in it, and (*c*) an effective authority behind it, in consequence of which, as generally obeyed, it becomes (*d*) a standard of behaviour. Then we take this word " law ", and apply it to the constitution of the physical world, where (*a*) it is not a personal command, nor a command at all, and (*b*) it has not any moral quality, and (*c*) it has not an effective authority behind it—unless we bring in a belief in God, and so pass from science to theology. All that is left of the conception with which we began is the notion of regular behaviour, and that is all that " a law of nature " can possibly mean, but very often men first of all leave out of consideration the question of origin altogether, and then, without realizing what they are doing, bring in the connotation of authority and enforcement, and proceed to argue as if, when you speak of any natural law, it means that this law *orders* things to act as they do, and *makes* them act as they do. It does not, of course; it merely states the fact that under certain conditions they *do* act thus.[2] If you want to explain why they do this you must begin to speak not of laws but of causes, and then you have deserted

[2] " To speak of natural laws as if the mere formula exerted a magical power over the phenomena and exacted something from them which did not follow of itself from their own nature is an empty rhetorical phrase. Laws can never be the causes of actual occurrences; they can only express the regular manner in which real things behave."—Sigwart, *Logik*, II, ü. 512.

science for philosophy. Now many of the difficulties that beset men's minds about the supernatural, about miracles, and providence, and prayer, arise from this quite illegitimate and indefensible sense of "law" in a phrase like "the laws of nature", which ought to mean merely the regular sequences of physical events, but into which there has been imported an anthropomorphic connotation which is here quite imaginative. The great scientists recognize this, but the confusion persists in the popular mind, and even in the minds of many religious thinkers who ought to know better. It is perfectly obvious, when you think it out, that a law of nature is merely a statement as to the normal behaviour of things in particular conditions; no more and no less. It does not ordain that things should happen thus; it does not compel things to happen thus; it simply states the fact that normally things do happen thus.[3] It is a statement of uniformity within definite limits, based upon observation, and expressed in metrical terms. As to why things behave in that regular way, or what makes things behave in that regular way, a natural law cannot tell you anything at all.

Whence comes the persistent fallacy, which haunts so many minds to-day, that the laws of nature are the explanation of events and even the cause of events? Obviously they are not, as every scientist and every logician of any eminence has repeatedly confessed. They are merely statements of the regular way in which things normally recur, when regarded from one particular point of view. Yet it is constantly assumed that when you have stated the natural law deduced from the recurrence you have named the cause of the recurrent fact, and explained it, and there is no more to be said. How does this delusion originate?

Doubtless in this way. As our knowledge extends we see ever more and more clearly not only that these laws of nature may be deduced from the facts everywhere in the universe,

[3] "Even though there were no assignable limits to the diversities existing in the absolute elements of things *per se*, and in their ultimate relations, yet a subject that could combine and select might still find its experience continuous and uniform."—James Ward, *Naturalism and Agnosticism*, p. 453.

and that they must eventually cover all reality, but also that they are all articulated, so to speak, fitting into each other in the most perfect way. Because you can deduce laws from the whole of nature, and these laws make an abstract system of thought which is self-consistent, it looks as if it is self-explanatory. The abstract system of laws answers so exactly to the facts that it looks as if it were the explanation of the concrete system of reality. It is natural and inevitable that it should answer exactly to the facts, because it was fitted to the facts in the first place, but we lose sight of that. It is rather as if you were to put together a jig-saw puzzle, and, as you find each piece fitting accurately into each other piece, come to the conclusion that the pattern of the pieces, as they fit each other, is the explanation of the puzzle. It is not: the explanation of the puzzle, in that sense, is the picture that the whole thing makes when the pieces have been put together. But if you forget for the moment that the picture was there before it was cut up into pieces to make a puzzle, and that the puzzle really exists in order to make the picture, you might be so impressed by the way that the pieces fit together as to think that the precise articulation of the pieces was really the explanation of the puzzle. Or, to change the illustration, the system of natural laws deduced by the human mind fits the system of reality as an intricate key fits an intricate lock. You are impressed by the fact that the complexity of the key corresponds with the complexity of the lock, and opens it. The thing works, and works simply, to all appearance, in spite of the complexity of the mechanism. That is rather striking, and you leap to the illogical conclusion that the key is the explanation of the lock. It is not, of course. The explanation of both the key and the lock must be that they were so designed and so manufactured as to be what they are, and, being what they are, to fit each other. Any real explanation of the universe must be sought along a similar line. The abstract laws of nature that have been constructed by the human mind fit the concrete reality of nature as it exists independently of us because one infinite intelligence is the source of both the world of nature and the mind of man.

A natural law then is not a cause, and not an explanation: it is an abstract rule relating to the regular behaviour of natural events. It is a summary statement of what will happen when some particular force is at work—if no other force is thought of as complicating and counteracting it. I say, if it is *thought of*, because in the world of fact there always are these complicating and counteracting factors, and especially where human action comes in. It is only in the world of thought that they can be ignored, for the time being, in order to get an abstract statement of regularity and necessity. So that it is strictly true to say that every natural law is an ideal statement, a pure abstraction, which does not and cannot represent the actual complexity of facts in the world, but only the ideal simplicity of one aspect of the facts, isolated in thought from every other aspect. The actual complexity of all the facts in nature at any moment could only be represented by the actual complexity of all the forces of nature operating together at that moment, and that immense and incalculable complication the human mind is utterly unable to entertain at one time, or to combine into one thought. If we are to have any conception of the universe as a regular system it can only be by way of isolating one particular aspect of things, and seeing that there is an ideal regularity in that isolated aspect. We carry on that mental process, and we find that this works well, both in theory and in practice, and as we do it with one aspect of things after another we conclude that there is an ideal regularity in the whole of things. Doubtless this is ideally true of the whole —that is to say, it is true of the whole in the infinite thought of God.[4] But it is certainly not true that there is any rigid regularity in the actual incidence of each natural law when found together with other natural laws, in this actual world, because then there is an almost infinite complex of interacting forces and laws, producing an almost infinite variety of actual results.

A natural law, then, is merely a statement as to the regular

[4] In the sense of Aristotle's definition of God as the νόησις νοήσεώς, " the knowledge of itself by knowledge ".

behaviour of things under certain conditions. We find that by careful observation of facts we can progressively deduce these regular codes of behaviour, as to everything in the world. All our modern knowledge, in the physical sciences and in other realms as well, is due primarily to that. Man has discovered in the modern period (or rather he has realized it to the full extent, for common sense has always taken it more or less for granted as a matter of practice) that it is a regular universe, where everything acts according to laws which can be depended upon, because *in the abstract* they are rigid and universal ; that is, it is inconceivable that they are ever absolutely infringed or that they ever become absolutely invalid anywhere in the universe. But that is a deduction from experience—a deduction which is the work of the human mind, and it ought never to be forgotten that the character of rigidity and universality which is attributed to physical laws is a pure abstraction in the mind. It simply does not exist in external fact. No physical law is really rigid or really universal in its actual operation, as a moment's thought is enough to show. If it were, that would mean in the case of the law of gravitation, for example, that every single thing in the world, at every single moment of time, is actually falling, with mathematical precision, toward the centre of the earth, which is certainly not the fact. The rigidity and the universality of the law are ideal, and not actual ; in the mind, and not in reality. That is to say, if you think of the law of gravitation as entirely isolated from every other law of the universe (which it never is in actuality) it means that theoretically a thing will fall in a straight line toward the centre of the earth, i.e. *it will do so as long as nothing else intervenes to hinder it.* And so with every other physical law. It is an abstract statement as to the behaviour of matter in one particular respect, when mentally isolated from every other fact. It defines what will happen, and happen necessarily and universally, as a matter of thought, in a purely ideal state of affairs, when everything except this particular law has been thought away. If nothing else is considered in the mind but the weight of an object and the attraction of the earth then it is necessarily and universally true, as an abstract principle, that the object will fall exactly toward the exact centre of the earth. But in practice this does not always happen, and one might say that strictly speaking it never happens at all, for it never happens with the absolute precision that the law prescribes, because there are other conditions and factors always present. Many things are not actually falling toward the earth now, because other laws and forces are in action preventing their fall, and of the things that do actually fall probably not one ever fell in an absolutely straight line toward the absolute centre of the earth, because there would be in every case, since the world began, some tremor of the earth, or some movement of the air, or some attraction by another object, or some other disturbing factor, that would create some minute deviation and result in the fall not being absolutely straight. As an abstract principle the law of gravitation is unchallengeable, but in the actual life of the universe it never acts alone, and therefore never acts undisturbed, and therefore never acts either with absolute rigidity or with absolute universality.

Both these points are extremely important. A natural law does not in reality act with absolute precision, since it is never absolutely isolated in its action, and therefore in actuality it is not, strictly speaking, rigid; and a natural law does not in reality act at every point and at every moment, since it is frequently impeded by the action of other laws. and therefore in actuality it is not, strictly speaking, universal. The rigidity and the universality are theoretical.

These considerations may be illustrated by the degree in which we are able to predict events in the physical world. It is because of the theoretical regularity and the theoretical universality of natural laws that we can predict physical events at all. It is because the regularity and universality are only theoretical, and not actual, that we can only predict any physical event approximately, with less than absolute precision, and that we cannot predict some physical events at all. So a chemist can predict the behaviour of several chemical substances when brought into contact with each other, if he already knows the properties and quantities of the substances, and if they are isolated from all other substances, in an experiment. He may be able to predict with what is relatively a minute accuracy, but obviously it is not absolute accuracy, for we know that if his instruments were more delicate, and his measurements more exact, he could predict with still more accuracy. He cannot predict at all the behaviour of an indefinite number of substances in conjunction outside the laboratory, for the simple reason that there would not then be that isolation from disturbing factors which is vital to a chemical test. A known quality of one substance might be changed or counteracted by an unknown quality of another substance. It is only by limiting the number of substances, and excluding interference by other substances, that he can predict their behaviour at all. In other words, physical results can only be forecast with imperfect precision, and on a limited scale, because the regularity and the universality of physical laws are not actual but ideal; in action the laws are not perfectly regular and in action they are not absolutely universal, because at every point their regular operation is affected, and their universal operation is limited, by the existence of other laws. Hence we cannot predict on the universal scale of events, because there the laws complicate each other still more, and only an infinite intelligence could predict what will happen in that widest range of all.

There is, as a matter of fact, an incalculable variety of ways in which things actually happen in the universe, but we can ignore the actual variousness and state that such and such a thing will happen in a perfectly regular way—*if* none of the other innumerable and incalculable possibilities happen to prevent it. But that *if* is always implicit in any statement as to the rigid and universal character of any natural law, and here, as elsewhere, there is much virtue in an *if*. Since the clock on the mantelpiece of my study is constructed in accordance with physical laws which are ideally regular and ideally universal, and since it is now a quarter to twelve, I can be quite sure that in fifteen minutes the clock will strike twelve—*if* in the interval I do not take it into my head to stop the clock; *if* the mainspring does not break, or any other part of the mechanism fail; *if* the maid in dusting the clock does not let it fall; *if* the house and everything in it are not thrown down and destroyed by an earthquake; *if*—a thousand other contingencies do not happen in the meantime.

By ignoring all these real contingencies I can make the definite statement that the clock will strike twelve, *but only by ignoring these contingencies*. And so it is throughout the physical universe. By ignoring all other factors, I can make a theoretical statement of a definite character as to what will happen in given physical conditions, and that statement is called a law of nature. But it is only a fixed and universal law in the sense that it is fixedly and universally true in these conditions, when all other conditions are ignored. It can be stated, in the form of a mental concept, as a principle of natural behaviour that is ideally inflexible in its operation and ideally universal in its range, and we find it extraordinarily useful, both in theory and in practice, but the inflexibility and universality only exist in a mental construction, and are only gained by eliminating the actual irregularity and the actual limitation that are found in the world of real events. A natural law is really like an average. If you state that as a matter of averages Englishmen marry women 2.05 years younger than themselves that does not mean that every Englishman must do so, or does so as a matter of fact,[5] but it reduces to a mean the almost innumerable differences of age that actually exist.

So an ideal regularity in one aspect of things, and even an actual regularity (if such existed) can coexist with an immense variety in the whole of things. A mosaic in an old church in Venice may consist entirely of minute squares of different colours. No one would be foolish enough to

[5] Cf. James Ward, *Naturalism and Agnosticism*, pp. 106-7, where it is pointed out, incidentally, that Buckle, the author of *The History of Civilisation*, did actually say that the statistics of suicide meant that, in a given state of society, within such and such a period, a certain number of persons *must* put an end to their lives!

argue that only one picture could possibly be constructed out of these, because each of the tesserae is fixed in shape and fixed in colour. Yet that is precisely parallel to what is done by all those who hold a doctrine of mechanistic determinism, and by all those who are subconsciously influenced by such a doctrine. The implicit argument is always that because the universe is governed by fixed laws things must happen in a fixed way, and could not possibly happen otherwise, and therefore prayer and providence and miracle are ruled out. Now going back to the illustration of the mosaic, it is obvious that with a very large number of pieces, though the form and the colour of each one is unchanged and unchangeable, the artist may produce an immense variety of designs, as the result of different arrangements of the pieces. So out of the varied groupings of ideally rigid laws an infinite variety of actual results may come, and indeed does come, from moment to moment, in the physical world.

We do not need to go beyond our own experience either to illustrate that or to prove it. All human activity means that we use regular forces, according to regular laws, none of which we can really change or cancel, to bring about the most varied and the most contradictory results. I can let a ball fall to the ground or I can throw it into the air. I can keep it in a fixed position, or I can keep it in constant motion, as long as my muscular energy holds out. I can place it where it will float on the water, or where it will burn on the fire. I have not infringed any physical laws in doing these contradictory actions :[6] I have merely rearranged the operation of various physical forces, setting them in motion so that they counterbalance one another in this way and in

[6] " When the human will acts upon the external world, and produces a sensible effect, it does not thereby violate any law of Nature. . . . Similarly, when God works a miracle, it is not supposed that any of the laws of Nature are suspended, but that God counteracts or modifies some of the effects which those laws would ordinarily produce, by a process analogous to that by which the human will acts upon and influences physical Nature. That is admitted by John Mill, who says, ' The interference of human will with the course of Nature is not an exception to law : and by the same rule interference of the divine will would not be an exception either '."—Charles Harris, *Pro Fide*, p. 264.

that. Practically everything that a man can do would serve equally well as an illustration. It is in accordance with natural laws that water flows downward, but when we use a pump we make it flow upward. That is no "violation" of natural law; it is no "interference" with nature, or "intervention" into nature—except in the sense that the will and the energy of man (which are already a part of nature, and which are exercised in the midst of a system of natural forces and natural laws) regroup those laws and forces into a different combination, and make them do the opposite of what they would do if they were left to themselves, without such human action. That, indeed, is what all human action amounts to, and surely it cannot be denied that God, if there be a God, can do what man can do, and can do it on an infinitely larger scale, and with infinitely stranger results.

There is an actual direction of natural forces and natural laws in human activity, and there must be a universal direction of forces and laws in the whole universe, if God exists. It is a fact that the forces and laws of nature are constantly rearranged into new combinations from moment to moment. What finally directs that changing pattern? Now this law is in action, as we say; now it is momentarily suspended by another law; now both are in action together; now both are momentarily suspended by the action of another group of laws, and so on. It may be objected that it is not strictly accurate to speak of one law being suspended by another law, since every law is really in force all the time. So, for example, it can be urged that when I hold a book up in my hand, and prevent it falling to the ground, the law of gravitation is not really counteracted, because I feel the weight of the book, which proves that the attraction of the earth is still there, and that the law of gravitation is still in action. That, of course, is true enough, but it only amounts to a matter of definition. If you say that the law of gravitation is still in force here, as in that sense it is, it is nevertheless the fact that it is in force in a different fashion, and that the event which results is different from what it would be if I did not hold the book up in my hand. If you insist that every natural law is in force all the time it remains true that a different result is brought about by a difference in the combination, and therefore in the combined action of the various natural forces at work in the event. The actual pattern of arrangement, in the way that all the natural laws and forces are grouped together and act together, cannot have been exactly the same, as a matter of fact, at any two moments in the history of the universe. It is perpetually changing, and consequently a universe ruled by ideally rigid laws is not actually a rigid universe at all, but is almost immeasurably elastic in its real happenings. There is nothing whatever, therefore, in the laws of nature, rightly understood, that is any hindrance to a belief in prayer and providence and miracle.

V

THE MECHANICAL UNIVERSE

V

THE MECHANICAL UNIVERSE

When we consider the mechanistic view of the universe, so largely held during the last few generations, an immediate and important distinction must be made. As an explanation of the origin and existence of the universe it is merely fantastic; as an abstract hypothesis to describe the actual working of the physical universe when once in being it is not only warrantable, but extraordinarily effective and extraordinarily convenient.

First, then, to think of the universe as a mere mechanism, and then to go on to think of that as a sufficient explanation of the universe, is more crudely anthropomorphic than any primitive myth about gods and demons, and yet it is not anthropomorphic enough. For to think of the universe as a vast machine is to think of it in terms of something that man has invented and that man has manufactured, since any and every machine is a product of human thought and human work. Why it should be regarded as reasonable to interpret the universe by the analogy of a machine, but dispensing with the thought of the intelligence that designed and the will that made the machine, is rather a mystery. But there it is, and it seems to satisfy many minds to regard the whole universe as a vast mechanism which, when once you accept it as such, needs no further explanation with regard to its origin, existence, and purpose.

But a mechanistic theory of the actual working of the material universe when once the universe is designed, energized and existent, is a very different proposition, and, in one sense, underlies all our modern science, as an intellectual theory. It is well to remember this—that the mechanistic view cannot possibly be a valid theory of origin, but may be a useful theory of action, though it will be found that these very different conceptions are frequently confused, and, in consequence, must here be discussed more or less concurrently.

There is one factor which largely accounts for the prevalence of the mechanical view of the universe in the popular mind. It is that we live in a mechanical age. One striking difference between the modern world and every previous period is that in the world we know human life has been largely changed by mechanism. If a Roman travelled to the remote island of Britain in the days of Nero he had to walk, or ride a horse, or drive a chariot, from Italy to the northern coast of Gaul. There were no other ways in which he could travel overland. So it was for almost the next two thousand years, and so it had been from the days of primitive man. Then, within the last hundred years or so, came the railway, the motor-car, and the aeroplane, and to-day you can fly from Rome to London in a few hours. That is a very striking development ; it is purely a development in mechanism ; and it has come about within three or four generations. No wonder that such changes have impressed, and almost obsessed, the mind of man, for there are a thousand other illustrations of the same kind of mechanical progress. It must be remembered, too, if we want to realize the imaginative impact of all this, that mechanism of any complicated kind is a very recent thing in human experience. Little more than a century ago a pump, a loom, a windmill, and a grandfather's clock were the most complicated machines known to men. Now every man is familiar with the steam engine, the electric motor, the typewriter, the telephone, and a hundred other applications of mechanical principles, and almost every man knows something of extremely complicated machines in factories. The minds of men in the present age, therefore, are familiar with the general notion of mechanism, and are disposed to employ the mechanical analogy in the interpretation of nature.

Now what is mechanical has two main characteristics. It *is* regular, and it *looks* automatic. First, all mechanical action, as compared with personal action, is regular. A man doing manual work tires, pauses, begins again, works faster or slower ; a machine runs untiringly, unceasingly, regularly, when once it is set in motion, unless something goes wrong with the mechanism. It is regular movement, regular action, for the machine has no muscles to weary in its work, and no will to change its action from time to time.

Second, mechanical action has at least the look of being automatic. We know that the machine has been designed and made by man and is started and stopped and supervised by man, but if we forget that as we watch it at work it seems to act by itself without any personal or voluntary direction at all. Now it is the fact of being regular, and the illusion of being automatic, that seem to make mechanism so facile an interpretation of nature. The machinery which is familiar to modern man acts with perfect regularity, in accordance with mechanical laws, and there is little apparent need for personal control or personal interference, for the most part. Then follows the thought that the whole of nature acts with the same exact regularity, in accordance with the same mechanical laws, and that here again there is no necessity to introduce any personal element. It is forgotten that the automatic machine in the factory, which seems to operate itself, was designed and made by men, and has to be controlled and repaired by men, and that in fact the very way in which it seems to dispense with intelligence is the most complete proof that there is intelligence behind it all. But if you forget to ask what designed, and made, and controls the mechanism of nature, you can hastily conclude that it is merely an automatic machine, and that there is no need for the hypothesis of God.

The plausibility of the mechanistic view of nature is due to the two facts that have been pointed out. A machine in its action is perfectly regular, and largely automatic. It has been expressly designed to be that. To be effective, it must work evenly and constantly, and it must not need alteration and adjustment from moment to moment. It has been constructed by a personal intelligence with the definite purpose of eliminating all irregularity, and as far as possible any personal attention or personal interference in its action. Now a very similar process takes place in our minds in the construction of a mechanistic view of the universe. We create an intellectual regularity out of the complexity of natural events, and in doing so we deliberately eliminate all irregularities, and all consideration of personal action or personal interference of any kind. We deduce laws from nature which, as we say, operate with mechanical regularity, and appear to operate quite automatically. Of course they do, for that is the very purpose of our intellectual construction of these laws. We posit laws which in the abstract are mechanically regular by deliberately ignoring any actual irregularities : we posit laws which in the abstract are mechanically automatic by deliberately ignoring any personal interferences. All these points are important.

First of all, these mechanical laws of nature are mental abstractions.[1] The world of reality is always concrete : it is complex, irregular, individual. But our intellectual account of the world of reality is always abstract :[2] it is simplex,

[1] "Roundly stated, the real is always concrete, the symbolic is always abstract. The real implies individuality more or less : the symbolic is always a logical universal."—James Ward, *Naturalism and Agnosticism*, p. 175.

"The seventeenth century discovered that the world could be represented with amazing success as a series of instantaneous configurations of matter, which determined their own changes and thus formed a logically closed circle, a complete mechanistic system. Idealistic minds from Berkeley to Bergson have revolted against this system, and, not understanding the real issue, usually got the worst of the controversy. There is an error, but not where it has generally been imagined to be. It is really the error that has been pointed out so often in this book, the error of mistaking for concrete reality the abstractions inherently necessary for science, the error which Whitehead calls the Fallacy of Misplaced Concreteness. Abstractions are necessary for analysis, but they involve the ignoring of the rest of nature and of experience, from which the abstractions are made. Thus they give an incomplete picture even of science, and a still more incomplete one of the whole of existence. The doctrine of deterministic mechanism only applies to very abstract entities, the product of logical analysis."—W. E. D. Dampier-Whetham, *A History of Science*, p. 479.

[2] Science "in proceeding to generalizations and laws confines itself exclusively, and of necessity, to the 'repeatable'; which involves elimination or ignoring of whatever there may be of idiosyncrasy and of the *einmalig*. The common and the repeatable are necessarily in some degree abstract; whence it follows that science isolates itself from history, and that the Nature which it studies is a skeleton or a diagram, as compared with the Nature constituted

regular, general. It must necessarily be so. Any account of the world that included all the actual variousness of it would have to be a mere transcript of the world, as multitudinous and varied and irregular as the world itself; and therefore not really a rationale of it at all. If it is to be a rational account of the world it must rationalize the world by regularizing it,[3] and that can only be done by successively selecting some one line of resemblance after another, and stringing things along that line, ignoring for the time being all the differences which actually exist. If I want to make a catalogue of my library it is plain that the catalogue cannot be a full description of the books, because that would mean a description of the size, shape, binding, type, and entire contents of every book from page to page and from line to line. That would be a mere transcription of all the books, as bulky as the library itself, and entirely useless. I must select some point of resemblance between the books, perhaps what is really a rather fortuitous and insignificant resemblance, such as that every author's name begins with some particular letter of the alphabet, and so I can make out a list where the authors' names are arranged in alphabetical order ; or perhaps what is a more organic and significant resemblance, such as that each book is on some particular subject, and so I can make out a list where the names of the books are arranged under the headings of theology, philosophy, science, and so forth. In any such catalogue all the other differences between the books are ignored, and only some one resemblance is used as the principle on which the books are assorted and listed. Everything else is disregarded except the detail, " The names of all

by the presentational continua of experients and by the behaviour and interactions of the world's real members."—F. R. Tennant, *Philosophical Theology*, I, pp. 337-8.

[3] " Materialism is the truth about any object, just in so far as the object is reducible to terms of pure mathematics ; and no object is so reducible except by consciously or unconsciously shutting our eyes to everything that differentiates it from anything else. This conscious or unconscious act of abstraction is the very being of the scientific consciousness, and it is therefore no matter for pained surprise when science shows a bias towards determinism, behaviourism and materialism generally."—R. G. Collingwood, *Speculum Mentis*, p. 168.

the authors of these volumes begin with A", or the detail "The subject of all these volumes is philosophy". It is only in some such fashion that a catalogue can be made at all, i.e. a list that will be short enough and orderly enough to be of any use. In other words, it must be summary, and it must be regular, and to be that it must be selective.[4]

It is precisely so with any scientific rationale of the universe. There is, for example, an immense variety of substances in the world, which differ in many ways, but we seize upon one main point of likeness, and classify them as mineral, vegetable, animal. There is an immense variety of animals in the world, which again differ in many ways, but we seize upon one main point of resemblance and classify them as mammals, birds, reptiles, fishes, and so forth. In each of these examples there is, of course, a real resemblance, but the point at the moment is that we have pitched upon one actual resemblance, and, for the purposes of classification, deliberately ignored all the other actual differences. When we say, for instance, that birds belong to the same genus we are selecting a particular aspect in which they resemble each other, so that this will serve, as it were, for a compartment in which to place this particular package of creatures. We do not mean that all birds are really altogether alike, for they differ as far as a sparrow differs from an ostrich: we mean that they are sufficiently like one another, in one particular way, to enable us to class them together and call them by the same name. And so with all the other facts of the universe.

For we do precisely the same thing when we speak of natural laws as when we speak of natural species. The only difference is that when we think of things in their static

[4] "Scientific knowledge is always the description of facts and their relations in general terms. It gives us knowledge of practical utility rather than understanding. It does not eliminate mystery; it merely puts it neatly away where we can turn our backs on it if we do not like it. . . . It is a sound rule of method to state a problem in the most general terms by a process of abstraction, and to simplify the data as much as possible. When the problem has been solved it is very tempting to assume that there are no further problems, and that the data that have been omitted for simplicity's sake do not exist."—A. D. Ritchie, *The Natural History of Mind*, pp. 13, 14.

relations we speak of species, and when we think of things in their dynamic relations we speak of laws. In other words we generalize what things *are* by the concept of species, or resemblances in kind, and we generalize what things *do* by the concept of laws, or resemblances in action. In each case we select some likeness between things, and disregard all the differences, and then say " these things are alike in this respect: they belong to the same species ", or " these things act alike in this respect: they follow the same law ". But the concept " species " does not *make* things alike: it simply states that in one respect they *are* alike, and the concept " law " does not *make* things act alike: it simply states that in one respect they *do* act alike. Exactly as we think of things belonging to the same species, because in one particular aspect they are alike, disregarding the many aspects in which they are not alike, so we think of things following the same law, because in one particular aspect they act alike, disregarding the many aspects in which they do not act alike. Things of one particular sort, when not prevented from doing so by any other force, behave in one particular way, and we say when they act in that way that it is an instance of some mechanical law (sometimes we even say that they " obey " that law, as if they had wills and were obeying a command—a piece of anthropomorphic thinking as bad as was ever charged upon either a savage or a theologian !) [5] All that the mechanical law means here is that some things, in some circumstances, resemble each other in their habit of behaviour; we have selected out of all the ways in which these things behave differently this particular way in which they behave alike, and instead of speaking of this as a natural habit, or some such phrase, we unhappily describe it as a

[5] " The current scientific terminology is full of such (i.e. metaphors and parables), and we only realize that we have been talking in similes when the progress of knowledge has enabled us to outgrow them. Thus we repudiate as fanciful the powers of Love and Hate working between the elements, as Empedocles represented ; though we still talk with little misgiving of attractive and repulsive forces, of chemical affinities and bonds ; speak of organisms acquiring and bequeathing, and of seeds and eggs as inheriting and so forth."—James Ward, *Naturalism and Agnosticism*, p. 246.

natural law—unhappily, because the word "law" brings in many entirely unwarranted connotations. But the important point here is, as was said before, that this concept of law does not make things act alike, any more than the concept of species makes things be alike: it merely states that in one particular respect they do act alike. We have abstracted, from all the irregularity of actual events, a general rule of mechanical regularity in regard to one aspect of their behaviour.

The device of numeration may serve as an illustration of the point. Numerical notation is one of the very greatest of human inventions, for all mathematical science has grown out of it. It began when early man discovered that it was often very useful to keep a reckoning of things by ticking them off on his fingers, which is the origin of all the systems of numeration. Very much later the Arabic numerals were invented, and if I write down the figure 5, or the figure 10, or a simple equation like $5+5=10$, it is really a summary, abstract, and convenient way of saying what early man meant when he said to himself that so many stones, or spears, or whatever primitive man wanted to count, made as many as the fingers on one of his hands; or as many as the fingers on both his hands; or that twice as many as he could reckon on the fingers of one hand made as many as he could reckon on the fingers of both hands.

That is to say, every arithmetical equation is a summary and abstract statement of relations between facts that could not be stated otherwise except in a fashion that is much more clumsy and much less useful. In numbers and figures man has devised a way in which such statements may be made much more simple, and, for the purposes of further reckoning, much more practicable.

But observe what the arithmetical statement is not, and does not profess to be. It does not offer a method which can give a full or adequate description of anything, for the things enumerated may differ enormously, and be anything from angels to frogs, or stars to potatoes. It is not a cause, for it does not produce the fact that the things are so many. It is not an explanation, for it does not tell us why the things are so many. It is simply a statement of fact, from one particular angle—that of number. It says that, disregarding the nature, and size, and shape, and colour, and value of these things and everything else that is characteristic of them, except the numerical relation, *these things are so many*, and then states that fact in the extremely convenient symbols that we call figures. That is all.

Now in a similar way every natural law is a short, compressed, useful, abstract statement of one aspect of fact. It reduces the actual variety of things to a level line of resemblance in one respect: it treats them, for one purpose, as if they were all alike, and equal members of a regular series. It does not give us a complete account of any of the events concerned. It does not make the thing happen so. It does not explain why the thing happens so. It states that normally, and as regards this one particular aspect of the thing, it does happen so. Every natural law is thus an abstract statement of some resemblance and recurrence in nature, some regularity which we have deduced from nature which looks mechanical because it is regular.

Then, moreover, we only arrive at the abstract and mechanical regularity of a natural law by ignoring both the possibility and the fact of any personal interference at any point. No natural law can be conceived as regular and universal in its action except theoretically, because in actuality and in action it is not regular, and it is not universal. All human action is, in one way or another, an interference with the normal action of natural laws, though the word interference is not a satisfactory one. But in every human act we do at least rearrange the incidence of natural laws, to make things happen that would not happen naturally, so to speak—that would not happen, at least, if nature were left to itself. Almost anything where nature and man are operating together will illustrate the point. We say, for example, that it is in accordance with the mechanical laws of nature that iron will sink in water. If you think of iron in its one aspect of a metal, and of water in its one aspect of a fluid, apart from any action on the part of man, we know that it is true that iron will sink in water. That is universally true, and necessarily true, as a matter of the laws of mechanics, when you are thinking only of iron merely as a heavy solid, and only of water merely as a tenuous liquid, and when you are not thinking of any personal action that affects the iron and the water. But, as a matter of fact, iron does not always sink in water. The iron may be suspended in the water by a chain, so that it cannot sink. It may be formed into a hollow vessel filled with air, so that it will actually float. The water may be under such pressure that it will force the iron upward, instead of letting it sink. The statement that iron sinks in water is therefore only true when you disregard all the conditions in which it does not do so—which sounds foolish enough, but really represents the actual state of the case. When you ignore all the other interfering factors, especially any human action (but equally, of course, any personal action by beings other than men, if such there be) and exclude all considerations except the weight of the iron and the fluidity of the water, it is true that iron will sink in water by the automatic action of mechanical forces and laws. The action is automatic simply in the sense that we have deliberately ignored all action that is not automatic. To get a statement of regular behaviour that shall be, in the abstract, perfectly regular and absolutely universal, we have excluded in our thought all possibility of personal action by God or by man, and are left with the conception of automatic mechanism.

Then this mechanistic conception of nature is reinforced by the double appeal, intellectual and imaginative, that it makes to our minds. First, the laws of nature operate, as we say, with mechanical regularity: in fact, of course, they are nothing more than statements of regularity, constructed by our minds, and imposed upon nature. Those laws, as they are mentally devised by us, make a system which is coherent and consistent, even if it is not complete, and as any new fact is discovered we generally see it falling into place in the system with mechanical precision. Here is what looks like, and in a sense really is, a mechanistic rationale of existence:[6] that is the intellectual fact which is so impressive. We have devised a scheme of apparent regularity and apparent necessity which fits in remarkably with the facts of the universe. Naturally it does so, because we have deliberately omitted in each aspect of regularity, all the irregularities, and in each aspect of necessity, all the contingencies.[7] We are amply justified in doing this. It is the only way in which we can get an understandable account of all the facts. It is quite true to say that a mechanical conception of the universe lies behind the scientific view, and that it is taking for granted this conception of uniform laws that are mechanical in character which has made all scientific progress possible since the days of Galileo, Newton, and Descartes. But it is important to consider carefully in what precise sense this is true. The scientist proceeds *as if* the universe were a mere mechanism, and *as if* there were no volition and no intelligence in the mechanism, because only so can he employ the theory of an abstract and absolute regularity. But this is not to say that there *is* no volition and no intelligence in the universal scheme: obviously there is, for there is the will and the intellect of man, to go no further than that for the moment. Human activity plays a part in the events of the universe, employing natural laws and natural forces to bring about results that would never have happened if the world of nature had been left to itself. But we must disregard the irregular and incalculable interference of humanity if we want to use an abstract rule of regularity that will give calculable results,

[6] "In some biological problems the organism must be treated as a whole, and this fact is of philosophical importance. But science is by its nature analytical and abstract, and is forced to express as much of its knowledge as possible in terms of physics, the most fundamental and abstract of all the natural sciences. When it was found that more and more could be so expressed, confidence was gained in the method, and there arose a belief that a complete physical or mechanical explanation of all existence is theoretically possible."—W. E. D. Dampier-Whetham, *History of Science*, p. xvi (Introd.).

[7] "Philosophical empiricism is born here, then, of a confusion between the point of view of intuition and that of analysis. Seeking for the original in the translation, where naturally it cannot be, it denies the existence of the original on the ground that it is not found in the translation."—Bergson, *Introduction to Metaphysics*, pp. 27-8.

and equally we must disregard any personal action by beings other than men. But that does not mean that we have denied the existence of any such activity: it only means that we deliberately disregard it for a special purpose. We have no right and no need to rule it out either as a creative activity at the beginning of the mechanism, or as a continuous activity from moment to moment during the existence of the mechanism. We only disregard any discontinuous and irregular activity of a personal and volitional kind in order to presume a continuity and a regularity upon which we can calculate. A watch is a mechanism, but I know that it was a man's brain and a man's will that designed it, and made it in the beginning, and that also, in a sense, operates it all the time, for it is not only true that a man winds it up, but also that the man who designed it provided in his design for a continuous motion, so that this motion is really as much the product of human volition as if a man moved the wheels around with his finger from moment to moment. So that there is a human intelligence and human will behind all the mere mechanical regularity of the watch. But more than that: the mechanical regularity of the watch's motion is merely presumed in thought, and does not always exist in fact. For you may deliberately stop the watch, or forget to wind it up, or alter the regulator so that the watch goes too fast or too slow, or otherwise interfere with the mechanism. All these things may happen, but if I want to assume that the watch will go regularly and keep time, I must assume that they do not happen. It is only by the assumption that these things do not happen—though they may, and often do—that I can reckon upon regularity in the motions of the watch. And it is precisely so with our employment of the concept of mechanism in the universe. We deliberately disregard all action that is not mechanically regular (though we know that there is action, at least on the part of man, that is irregular and incalculable) in order to be able to use the extraordinarily serviceable concept of mechanical regularity. There is an impressive coherence and consistency about the whole method and the whole conception. It unifies and regularizes and rationalizes the world, and enables us, as we say, to understand it, that is, to see everything fitting into its place in a mental scheme of regular relations and regular recurrences. But we ought not to forget what we must have done in devising this method—we should remember that we have attained an abstract and artificial regularity which looks mechanical, merely because it has omitted all that is not mechanical.[8] And we ought not to think that our mechanical laws explain anything, for they do not, any more than a chart of the Atlantic explains the existence of the currents that are found in that ocean.

Then there is added to the purely intellectual appeal made by the conception of an abstract regularity of laws which always appear to fit together with a predestined accuracy,

[8] " The universe may be completely mechanical when viewed from the abstract standpoint of mechanics, and yet completely spiritual from the aspect of the mind. A ray of star-light may be traced by physics from its distant source to its effect on an optic nerve, but when consciousness apprehends its brightness and colour and feels its beauty, the sensation of sight and the knowledge of beauty certainly exist, and yet they are neither mechanical nor physical."—W. E. D. Dampier-Whetham, *A History of Science*, p. xx (Introd.).

" It has gradually dawned upon me that the reason why philosophers who are well acquainted with physical or dynamical science are apt to fall into the error of supposing that mental and vital interference with the material world is impossible, in spite of their clamorous experience to the contrary (or else, on the strength of that experience, to conceive that there is something the matter with the formulation of physical and dynamical laws) is because all such interference is naturally and necessarily excluded from scientific methods and treatises.

" In pure mechanics, 'force' is treated as a function of configuration and momentum : the positions, the velocities, and the accelerations of a conservative system depend solely on each other, on initial conditions, and on mass ; or, if we choose so to express it, the co-ordinates, the momenta, and the kinetic energies, of the parts of any dynamical system whatever, are all functions of time and of each other, and of nothing else. In other words, we have to deal, in this mode of regarding things, with a definite and completely determinate world, to which prediction may be confidently applied.

" But this determination is got *by refusing to contemplate anything outside a certain scheme :* it is an internal truth within the assigned boundaries, and it is quite consistent with psychical interference and indeterminateness, as soon as these boundaries are ignored ; determinateness is not part of the *essence* of dynamical doctrine, it is arrived at by *the tacit assumption that no undynamical or hyperdynamical agencies exist :* in short, by that process of abstraction which is invariably necessary for simplicity, and indeed for possibility, of methodical human treatment."—Sir Oliver Lodge, *Life and Matter* (1905), pp. 161-2. (The italics are mine.)

the imaginative appeal which results from practical experience. We find that these laws deduced and abstracted from nature, provide us with rules of practice which are most effective. When the engineer who is building a bridge over a river applies to the work of construction the laws of mechanics that he has learned from his text-books he finds that those laws work. And our actual experience that these laws are mechanically dependable is the fact which is so imaginatively impressive. This is greatly stressed by the immense achievements of applied science—all the result of the assumption that mechanical laws may be depended upon in practice. The most ignorant man knows that the motor-bus in which he rides to work every day is constructed in accordance with our knowledge of mechanical laws, and could not be constructed otherwise, and that this is the clue to its effectiveness.

Then the unthinking man (and sometimes a real thinker who ought to know better) says or suggests, in effect, " These mechanical laws of nature, which are so impressive a system when thought of in the abstract, and which are so strikingly verified when we employ them as our rule in mechanical achievements—these laws are the explanation of all existence ".

It almost looks as if they were, while we are under the intellectual and imaginative spell of their abstract regularity and their mechanical effectiveness, until we remind ourselves that they have been deduced from reality by the human mind, and are mental generalizations as to the behaviour of nature, which are no more the cause or the reason or the explanation of things than a barometer is the cause or the reason or the explanation of the changes in the weather. If we want the cause and the reason and the explanation of things we must look to forces rather than to laws, to purpose rather than to mechanism, and finally to whatever it may be that creates the forces and originates the purpose. But if there is anything creative and anything purposive in the universe that ultimately means God, and if there be a God He can guide and guard my life, and hear and answer my prayer, and give the strangest tokens of His presence and power in the world that He made and that He rules.

VI

THE TRANSCENDENTAL REACTION

VI

THE TRANSCENDENTAL REACTION

It should be pointed out that most of the arguments against the supernatural which have been considered hitherto are, strictly speaking, superannuated, for they are all based upon a scientific philosophy that is definitely out of date, though these prejudices still haunt the minds of many. The materialist, mechanist, determinist conception is already hopelessly discounted, as an explanation of the universe, and we have begun to see the intellectual currents flow in another direction—a direction far more favourable to religion generally, and to the supernatural element in it particularly. It is interesting to notice this drift of thought in the present day.

The overwhelming fact in the intellectual life of men during these latter generations has been the dominance of the physical sciences. The world has been greatly preoccupied, for a considerable time past, with the study of the properties of matter. A vast mass of assured and priceless knowledge has resulted. But it is important to remember that in the wider ranges of pure thought it is not, so to speak, the actual results of science that are most influential. When these are established they are accepted ; they have their reactions upon our departmental knowledge, and there it ends. The ultimate problems are the same as they were before modern science began, exactly as the greater experiences of human life are unchanged by all the changes in our civilization which science has brought about. Birth and death, joy and sorrow, hope and fear, are very much the same things in ancient Greece and in modern England, despite all that has happened between Archimedes and Edison. And the final problems of thought, as to the origin and destiny and significance of the whole of existence, are pretty much what they have been ever since men began to think about these things at all.

Where the results of science are important in the general world of thought is mainly that they predispose the minds of men to accept the speculations of scientists, whether these are warrantable or not. The man in the street would be as contemptuous of Einstein and relativity as he generally is of philosophy and theology, except for this—he sees all around him the marvels of applied science. Here is real and wonderful evidence of what science can do, and therefore he is ready to take the word of scientists for abstract theories that would otherwise seem ridiculous. Apart from this it is not the actual and assured results of science that matter most in our wider thinking. It is rather what is often called the scientific view of the universe—the way of thought that stresses the uniformity of nature and the universality of law, and that often (venturing into more debateable regions) proceeds to teach a doctrine of mechanism or materialism, and then, in consequence, of determinism. Really that kind of thing is not science at all: it is a philosophical view of existence often held by scientists in the past, and supposedly based on science. It is regarded with more respect than it deserves for the reason previously suggested—the solid and marvellous results of science in its own sphere predispose our minds to take seriously a view of things which is supposed to be scientific.[1] But there is nothing scientific about it except that it has often been the only philosophy of scientific men. For, of course, it is philosophy and not science. To speak paradoxically it is the metaphysics of the physicist who does not believe in metaphysics. It is a philosophical interpretation of the universe which operates from the physical angle alone. It therefore naturally deals with the physical side of things—with development rather than origins or ends, with the process rather than the purpose or the value of the process, with the detailed way in which things happen rather than the why and wherefore of their happening. This is characteristic of scientific method, and therefore science, properly so called, never gives an ultimate explanation of anything, nor, if it knows it own business, does it profess to

[1] Dampier-Whetham, *History of Science*, p. 216.

do so. As Karl Pearson once expressed it, " an explanation is never given by science: the whole of science is description." What science can do is to examine things minutely and then classify them as more or less like and unlike other things, and so catalogue them into related series. The very business of science is with descriptive classification; the only sense in which it explains is that as things are sorted out into connected series we see them falling accurately into place and have the deepening conviction that there is a real scheme of the universe and that finally all things must fall into one regular and universal series. But that, while it shows that there is a rational order in the universe, in no way explains either the origin or the meaning of the universe. The reason why science can give no ultimate explanations is plain when you think it out. Science is the method of description by experiment, and experiment depends upon measurement of some sort. In fact, as Sir Oliver Lodge once put it, "Science is the metrical knowledge of phenomena". Now that kind of method can only give you a quantitative view of things. If it deals with qualities it can only deal with the quantities of qualities, so to speak. It cannot measure, and therefore cannot render any account of the real essence of any qualitative existence, nor of the real cause of anything at all. It can describe the physical antecedents and accompaniments, and nothing more, because there is nothing more in the way of material and therefore measureable facts. It is perfectly obvious, one would think, that while you can measure a physical fact or a physical process you cannot do that with ultimate causes, or ultimate results, or the validity that really depends upon these. Apply the tests of physical science, for example, to literature or to music. You can give a more or less scientific account of the growth of language, because that is a process with physical accompaniments that can be more or less measured. You can give a more adequate scientific account of the facts of mere sound, because these make a physical series that can be more accurately measured. But you cannot give any merely scientific account of what is really essential in Shakespeare or in Bach. As Professor

Eddington has shrewdly put it: " Beauty and melody have not the arithmetical pass-word and so are barred out. This teaches us that what exact science looks out for is not entities of some particular category, but entities with a metrical aspect."[2]

It is as if you were to measure the height and calculate the weight of the stones as you climb the tower of a cathedral, which, of course, is a perfectly legitimate and valid process. But it does not in any way explain the fact that the door by which you enter on the ground is Norman, and that the vaulting in the next stage is Early English, and that when you pass the clerestory the windows are in the Perpendicular style of the fourteenth century. The one progression does not explain the other. No doubt they are related, but they are not related in such a way that the one series is the sufficient cause and the adequate explanation of the other series. The metrical description which is all that can be given of the material series does not account for another accompanying set of facts where human perceptions of beauty come into consideration. Somebody once said that a Beethoven string quartet was only " the scraping of horses' tails upon cats' bowels ". Now that is a perfectly accurate description, as far as it goes. Considered as a mere series of sounds the music is undoubtedly produced by the friction of horsehair upon catgut. But the description is a woefully inadequate one, for all that. It only takes account of the more gross and more elementary facts, on the physical side. Contrast with that description the noble words of Newman about music : " Yet is it possible that that inexhaustible evolution and disposition of notes, so rich, yet so simple ; so intricate, yet so regulated ; so various, yet so majestic, should be a mere sound, which is gone and perishes ? Can it be that those mysterious stirrings of heart, and keen emotions, and strange yearnings after we know not what, and awful impressions from we know not whence, should be wrought in us by what is unsubstantial, and comes and goes, and begins and ends in itself ? It is not so ; it cannot be."[3]

[2] *The Nature of the Physical World*, p. 105.
[3] *Sermons preached before the University of Oxford*, pp. 346-7.

Now the measureable necessarily means the repeatable and the repeated. If there were only one material object in the whole universe it would be quite meaningless to say that it was an inch long or a mile long. It is only because there are many things in the universe, and because they are things which happen in recurrent series, and are therefore more or less alike, that we can compare them with each other, measure them by each other, and so allocate them their position and proportion in space and time. Science could give no account whatever of a unique thing, and as things approach the unique science fails to give any adequate account of them. If there is ever such a thing as a miracle, for example, science cannot fit it into the scheme of recurrence and comparison and measurement, and therefore has nothing to say of it. If a scientist were confronted with an undeniable miracle, all that he could say would be : " Here is a unique fact in the presence of which my methods are useless. Doubtless it is governed by some law, though the law entirely escapes my knowledge. Doubtless it falls into place, somehow and somewhere, in the regular scheme of universal existence, but I cannot see how and where, for I cannot fit it into any recurrent series known to me, and that is all I have to say."

Moreover the measureable necessarily means the analysable. If you are to give a metrical account of anything, that thing must be discrete, divisible into parts, capable of analysis. Now since science can only reckon with things as analysable, it can never account for the whole of things as a whole. It assumes the existence of the whole of things, and does not attempt to deal with the why and wherefore of the whole. It cannot take account of causation in any absolute sense, because that involves the interconnected relations of the whole universe. It can give some statement of what things are within the existing scheme of the universe, which is taken for granted. But it is often forgotten that the definite existence of every individual fact depends upon the existence of the universal scheme. Nothing whatever could exist as it does unless there were not only a mere totality, so to speak, but an organized totality. That is true in a degree of every single thing that can be called a whole. It is precisely Aristotle's point that a severed hand is not really a hand. The hand is a hand only in connection with the whole body, as a part of it, as a detail in the organization of the entire organism. And what is true of every relative whole must be even more true of the universe, the absolute whole. Now any analysis of a whole into parts, or any synthesis of parts into a whole, fails to reckon with precisely that—the causal organization of the whole, without which there would be no whole and therefore no parts of the whole. It is as if you were to analyse a poem into words, or to analyse a living body into chemical constituents, and then forget that without mind the words would never have been ordered into a poem, that without life the chemical constituents would never have been organized into a body. There is something in the whole which is not a mere adding together of the parts, something which makes the whole into a whole, and therefore makes the parts, which exist as parts of the whole. As an eminent psychologist has written in an important book: "We are beginning to see that organization pervades nature everywhere; that we cannot validly conceive an atom of any sort going about with all its properties and causal efficacy within it. Everything is bound up in a web of causal relations without which it is not; to conceive it as existing without such relations is to misconceive it. Neither a physical atom, nor a sensation, nor a soul, may be validly conceived as a pure and simple substance which takes part in events by entering into relations with other self-contained entities. In other words, relations are constitutional or constitutive of things; and organization is universal and primordial, not something superadded, suddenly or gradually, to a world of things that might have existed without it." [4]

Hence science cannot give any adequate account of the whole of existence, nor any really adequate account of anything. For to deal with phenomena as merely recurrent and measureable, partial and analysable, is not really to give any complete account of them. It is as if a statistician

[4] McDougall, *Modern Materialism and Emergent Evolution*, pp. 72-3.

insisted that there was nothing more to be said or explained about the English population when once he had tabulated the number, sex, and age of the inhabitants of the island. That is a true account as far as it goes, but it does not cover all the ground. There is much more that remains to be said, and it is much more essential and explanatory.

This inevitable inadequacy of scientific method is being realized more and more by the real thinkers of this generation. The result is interesting and important. We are witnessing a reaction from the merely scientific habit of mind, and that may be clearly discerned both in those who may be called scientific philosophers and in those who may be called philosophical scientists. It is impossible to survey these tendencies in any great detail here. We can only briefly indicate how they all appear to illustrate what is essentially the same general movement of thought.

First, some eminent philosophers who have been largely dominated by the scientific view have been forced to make allowance for what mere science does not explain, and what supposedly scientific theories of the mechanist and materialist type do not really admit at all. It is true enough, of course, that dogmatic materialism of the old-fashioned sort, which was associated, fifty or sixty years ago, with the names of Huxley and Spencer, is as dead as Queen Anne. It has been discredited for all serious thinkers for at least a generation past. Still, much of the habit of thought has remained, here and there. Of late years, however, many of the philosophers who are most influenced by science, and whose orientation would otherwise be toward a purely mechanist view, have realized that some account must be given of what is not merely quantitative, recurrent, and analysable—of the new, original, unique facts and qualities that appear in the history of the universe.

Hence, very largely, one of the most interesting movements in modern philosophical thought—the philosophy of Emergent Evolution. It is important to remember that it is intended to be definitely and decisively a philosophy of naturalism. As Professor Lloyd Morgan has said : " Not only atoms and molecules but organisms and minds are susceptible of treatment by scientific methods fundamentally of the same kind ".[5] There is not meant to be any place for the God of the theist, nor indeed for anything that does not fall definitely and wholly within a system of naturalism at the beginning, whatever may emerge from it before the end. But the philosophy of Emergent Evolution does at least see that the old mechanistic naturalism is not enough, and it recognizes that there are not only " resultants " but " emergents ". The emergent is a resultant, so to speak, but it is more. It is not merely the sum of the preceding conditions, for in addition to this there is something which is new, unforeseen and unforeseeable until it happens ; something which has not appeared before, and which is not explained by what has appeared before. This is a genuine attempt to make room for the facts in the life of the universe which are novel, and which are unpredictable because they are hitherto unparalleled and unrepeated. Obviously there are such facts. Oxygen combines with hydrogen, and there is the emergence of water, with its peculiar properties, which are not discoverable in oxygen and hydrogen in their pure state. At a particular stage in the history of the universe a new complexity arose in a system of atoms, and there was the emergence of life, with all its peculiar attributes of growth, and assimilation, and reproduction—qualities, again, which are not discoverable in the inorganic elements which go to make the material basis of life. At a still later stage in the development of the universe still further complexity arose in living organisms, and there was the emergence of consciousness, which, once again, is a new attribute, not to be discovered in the mere elements of the living organism.[6] Now here in each case is something novel and original, which could not have been predicted merely from what has gone before ; something *more*, which is not a mere totalized result of the antecedents. Something has happened which is analogous to what Browning says of the creative gift of the musician:

[5] *Emergent Evolution*, p. 2.
[6] Cf. McDougall, *Modern Materialism and Emergent Evolution*, p. 114.

"And I know not if, save in this, such gift be allowed to man,
That out of three sounds he frame, not a fourth sound but a star".

It is this unforeseeable and unaccountable appearance of the new which is meant by emergence. But does the mere phrase "emergence" really explain anything? It admits the novelty of the fact, but that is all. Where does the new thing emerge *from?* Surely it must emerge from either the outside or the inside of the system, and from either the past or the present of the system, so to speak. The inevitable logic of the situation, one would think, leads either to Theism or at least to Deism—either there is a creative spirit within the world of nature now, or there was a creative spirit beyond the world of nature at the beginning. Indeed, Professor Lloyd Morgan has gone very near to something like this, although he carefully avoids any language that would sound theistic. He admits that there is needed "something in the nature of a relating and directive Activity of which the *de facto* relatedness and the observed changes of direction (with which science is concerned) are the manifestation". "I use the word 'Activity' in this sense", he adds, "as the most non-committal name I can select. I write it with a capital letter to differentiate the concept as other than naturalistic . . . I frankly accept Activity under my third acknowledgement—one that supplements, but is nowise contradictory to the concepts of naturalism in its accredited domain." [7]

But an acknowledgement of this kind stands rather apart. One cannot help feeling that this is not what the philosophy of Emergent Evolution is really after. The general impression left upon the mind is that philosophers of this school want to say "emergence", and then leave it at that, as a way of escape from mechanism on the one hand, and teleology on the other. It is a system of naturalism which has been driven to admit that mere naturalism is not enough, and that there is an "x" expressed by the phrase "emergence". But you

[7] *Contemporary British Philosophy*, I, p. 304.

do not account for a thing's emergence by merely saying that it emerges.[8] As Tertullian said of another problem, *Unde ? et quare ? et quomodo ?*

Then some eminent scientists who have the philosophical mind have themselves begun to proclaim the bankruptcy of the merely scientific view. It really began with the new view of matter. The older science regarded mass as not only the main characteristic of matter as known to the senses, but as an original and final and ineradicable property of matter. Now that conception has gone. As Professor Whitehead has said, " We have got rid of matter with its appearance of undifferentiated endurance." [9] Matter is no longer regarded as a kind of gross solidity that can never be got rid of: a stuff made of atoms which are themselves solid, which might indeed be arranged in patterns of different density, as solids, liquids, gases, but which always and everywhere remained as minute particles of solidity. To-day matter is regarded by scientists as a kind of pattern of energy. In the words of Professor Mackenzie: " It is now generally recognized that the ultimate constituents of all material bodies have to be regarded as centres of electro-magnetic influence; and that no properties can be assigned to them except that of being such centres of action. The result of this is to break down the old distinction between matter and energy. We may say either that matter is nothing but a more or less persistent localization of energy; or that energy is a sort of ultimate matter." [10] There has been, in fact, a *bouleversement* of the general conceptions with which science operates. These are valid enough for all practical purposes, of course, but they

[8] " The recently prevalent fashion of talking freely about ' emergent ' evolution, as though the adjective could take the place of an explanatory theory, is a glaring illustration in point. The epithet is tantamount to an open confession that there is something really present in historical processes which ought not to be there if the substantive really means what it says. Something has ' come out of ' an alleged act of antecedent conditions which was never in the conditions and therefore is not rationally accounted for by specifying them, though we are still to pretend, by the use of an adjective, that it has been accounted for."—A. E. Taylor, *The Faith of a Moralist*, II, p. 67.

[9] *Science and the Modern World*, p. 55.

[10] *Ultimate Values*, p. 28.

can no longer be regarded as really ultimate and therefore really explanatory. The assumptions which science quietly took over from common sense (for that is what it amounts to) are now proved by the progress of science itself to be only working assumptions, approximations to some reality the absolute character of which escapes the scientific method. "The progress of science", Professor Whitehead writes, "has now reached a turning point. The stable foundations of physics have broken up .... The old foundations of scientific thought are becoming unintelligible. Time, space, matter, material, ether, electricity, mechanism, organism, configuration, structure, pattern, function, all require re-interpretation. What is the sense of talking about a mechanical explanation, when you do not know what you mean by mechanics?" [11] All the final conceptions of physical science are turning out to be paradoxes and antinomies. The scientist may be said, for example, to have reduced everything to motion, only to find that there is nothing left to move. But even if we disregard the element of paradox in the theories of advanced physics it remains true that the physicist's ultimate conceptions of matter and motion now appear to be at least unknown entities. Professor Eddington has summed up our scientific knowledge in the epigram: "Something unknown is doing we don't know what—that is what our theory amounts to." [12] The ultimates of science, in fact, are all passing out into a region of abstraction where only philosophers and theologians have any right of entry, or any means of exploration.

It is not that the real and magnificent results of science are in any way invalidated. The scientific method works all right on the lower level; for all pragmatic purposes it is perfectly valid and perfectly sufficient. But the scientist has discovered his limitations. He has found that he has no sort of ultimate knowledge, and therefore nothing on which to base a merely scientific *Weltanschauung*. You cannot very well have a materialist philosophy when you do not know

[11] *Science and the Modern World*, p. 23.
[12] *The Nature of the Physical World*, p. 29.

what matter is, or a mechanist philosophy when you do not know what motion is, or a naturalist philosophy when you do not know what nature is. You may try to reduce everything to matter and motion, but only to find in these days that matter and motion evaporate into nobody knows exactly what. You may attempt a philosophy of naturalism, only to find that the system of nature finally dissolves into what are really metaphysical conceptions. The scientist has discovered, in fact, and discovered by his own researches, especially in the region of mathematical physics, that *omnia exeunt in mysterium.*

Let it be clearly understood that nothing whatever has been said here against science and scientific method properly understood. The argument is simply that science has its limits in the very nature of what it is, and that while it is always right to begin with the empirical facts and to operate with the experimental method, you cannot stop there. By all means measure all that is measurable, and analyse all that is analysable, but when that is done you must go on from the facts to the significance and purpose and value of the facts; from the mechanical to the teleological; from the natural to the transcendental; from all that is measurable by our standards and expressible in our terms to the immeasurable and the inexpressible—in short, from the merely scientific view (right as it is in its own way) to the more universal view of philosophy and theology. Here is a transcendental reaction, for both metaphysics and dogmatics are coming to their own again; in the future metaphysics will be no longer almost submerged by psychology, and dogmatics will be no longer almost surrendered for historical criticism and the study of the origins of religion. Apologetics need not be so timid in these days, for if the defenders of the faith could only see it the whole tendency of modern thought is far more favourable to orthodoxy than it has been for several generations past. The dogmatic materialism of the nineteenth century is dead, and it is easier to accept the supernatural in religion than it has been at any time during the last two centuries. For we can far more readily conceive of a real activity of God in a universe which is ultimately a great manifestation of energy, than in a universe where there seemed to be an almost impassable gulf between mind and matter, as matter was conceived by the science of fifty years ago—matter with its look of " undifferentiated endurance ". The science and the philosophy of our own generation now leave a wide opening (to say the very least) for faith in miracle and providence and prayer.

VII

MIRACLE

VII

MIRACLE

It is often suggested that men found little difficulty in believing in miracles until the scientific view of the universe came to prevail in modern times, because until then the conception of a reign of law had not dawned upon the mind of man.[1] That surely needs some considerable qualification. Common sense has always assumed some regular connection between cause and effect, and indeed human life would have been impossible without that assumption. If prehistoric man had not believed that when he sprang into the air he would normally come down again to the ground he would never even have ventured to jump across a puddle, and if he had not known that a missile would normally travel in the direction in which it was thrown, and not backwards or sideways, and would travel further as he used more of the strength of his arm in throwing it, he would never have been able to bring down his prey by flinging a stone or a spear at it. Some regular causation, some dependable action of forces, must be presumed by the most primitive of mankind in the most ordinary actions of life. This inference, which results from the most elementary experience, is really, of course, the foundation of all science and all philosophy, and it exists, practically as an instinct, in the life of man in its very early stages.

It is therefore an exaggeration to regard the conception of a reign of law as wholly modern, and to attribute the difficulty about miracle to that. Everything that would be a miracle to us in the twentieth century would have been a miracle to prehistoric man, though that is not true the other way round,

[1] Here is a point where my argument resembles that of Dr. C. S. Lewis in *Miracles*, p. 58, and there are several other close parallels. I must therefore say that this book was completed three years before Dr. Lewis's volume was published. I congratulate myself on the fact that my line of thought should have often coincided with that of so brilliant a thinker and writer as Dr. Lewis.

for many things that would have been miraculous to prehistoric man are not miraculous to us, because the frontier of knowledge has been greatly extended, and much that would have been supernatural to man in early days has now been ranged under natural laws. As a matter of fact things happen in the natural world in much the same way in every age, and some of them seem stranger than others, but while early man attributed some of these events to the action of gods and demons, modern man attributes all of them to the action of laws and forces. On a close analysis the one explanation is as anthropomorphic as the other, and as defective. What is essential in each is really needed to supplement the other —that is to say, the thought of direction by will and intelligence (which is what early man crudely intended by gods and demons) is needed to supplement the thought of automatic regularity (which is what modern man often means by laws and forces) as much as the other way round. In other words, to think of anything happening either automatically or arbitrarily is equally unsatisfactory.

A century hence it will probably seem a very strange fact to anyone who surveys the thought of the previous hundred years that it was so largely dominated by the mechanical, and that the personal was at such a discount. Any conception of personal action and personal direction in the universe, apart from humanity, has become foreign to the modern mind. To think of any direction of events by angels, for example, would seem quite fantastic to nearly everyone to-day, and to think of any such direction by God seems almost as difficult for many people. But to conceive of the whole of existence as a mindless mechanism would now appear perfectly rational to perhaps the majority of men. When you think this out in a detached and disinterested way it will be seen to be purely a modern prejudice, and an entirely irrational one.

It is quite true that what has really made all our modern knowledge of the universe has been the deliberate exclusion of arbitrariness (such as a belief in the action of gods and demons suggests) from our scientific conception of the working of the universe, but it must be remembered that it is not merely such supernatural agency that is put out of our thoughts when we think in terms of physical science, but all human agency as well. We find it extraordinarily useful to think of the physical universe *as if* there were no personal or volitional activity in it, because in that way, and only in that way, we can reduce the behaviour of nature to rules which are, in the abstract, perfectly regular and absolutely universal. We could not envisage any natural law as regular and universal in its operation, for example, if we were actually taking into account at the moment the numberless instances in which man's will diverts its operation by bringing some other law into action. It is only by deliberately ignoring every such case of action or direction by man, and *equally of action or direction by any other will or intelligence*, that we can represent the course of nature as strictly regular, and the laws of nature as strictly universal. Hence, of course, the illusion of automatic action in the natural world. We have put out of our minds, deliberately, for the sake of getting a regular, metrical, mechanical account of the world, the thought of all intelligent direction and all personal action, and find ourselves left merely with the thought of an automatically regular universe which operates itself (and which apparently made itself, though the problem of its origin is seldom thought about, and still seldomer thought out logically). If we want such an account of the physical universe in metrical and mechanical terms, as for the purposes of science we do, we must exclude from that account all intelligence and purpose, human or other; but we ought to remember that we have done this, and that a really complete account of the universe must include those supremely significant factors that, for a special purpose, we have deliberately left out.

This deliberate exclusion of the disturbance introduced by personal action in order to get a statement of regularity in the shape of a natural law, is parallel in a way with what we do when we reduce any series of facts in human life to an average. It is the elimination of variations in order to get a summary and generalized statement of the facts. Thus actually in our English population males die at any age from under a year to over a hundred years, and the number of those who live for exactly the same period is comparatively small. But we eliminate all these innumerable differences by condensing them into a mean, and state that the average lifetime of males in England is 57 years, which, of course, does not mean that every English male lives so long and no longer, and must live so long and no longer. But it is very useful to be able to express many facts in the life and behaviour of men in averages, thus treating human experience for the moment as if it could be reduced to exact measurements and precise statistics, which it certainly cannot be, except by ignoring or cancelling out all the irregularities.

And so in our conception of natural laws. We have deliberately cancelled out all the actual variations in natural events, in order to make a summary statement which shall be true, as a pure abstraction, and only as a pure abstraction, of the behaviour of things in one particular aspect, and only in one particular aspect, when isolated in our thought from all else. A natural law does not mean that a natural event happens in every case precisely according to that law and that law alone, and that it cannot possibly happen otherwise. But it is very convenient to have a generalized statement—ruling out for the moment all the actual irregularities—as to the behaviour of natural events regarded in the abstract, and in one particular aspect.

Then, having reached this interpretation of the universe as a system of regular laws, the conception of miracle is held to be all but impossible, because it would be an arbitrary interposition into this system of regularity. A miracle is, of course, an interposition in one sense—it is an unfamiliar fact interposed in our experience of familiar facts. But more than this is meant by the use of such words, for the suggestion always is that a miracle is a fact intruded into the natural order, and contravening it. Indeed, it seems impossible to discuss miracle without the suggestion being made sooner or later that a miracle would necessarily be an "interference" or an " intervention " on the part of the Deity. It cannot possibly be that, of course, either from the scientific or from the theological point of view. The theologian would have to object quite as strongly as the scientist to such an impossible conception. Yet it is always reappearing, and sometimes it is met with in the writings of responsible thinkers who really ought to know better. The whole notion of " interference ", and " intervention ", and " breach of law ", and so forth ought to be dismissed immediately and permanently from our thoughts. There can be no " interference " except in the sense that every natural law is perpetually interfering with every other, and no " intervention " except in the sense that every natural cause is perpetually intervening in some new grouping of causes. There can be no " breach of law " ; a natural law cannot be broken. The very phrase is another illustration of the unfortunate use of " law " in a misleading way, for a moral law or a human law may be broken, but a law of nature cannot be, for it is simply the concept of an absolute regularity of recurrence, and obviously if that recurrence were broken at any point it would not be absolutely regular, and the natural law would not be a natural law at all.

It is plain that any conception of " interference " or " intervention " would be meaningless unless it meant first of all that there was a regular system with which to interfere, an established order in which to intervene. Then it is implicitly denied that this system, this order, is energized and directed by God, for if it were there would be no need for Him to interfere and intervene. If the whole of the universe is being actively controlled, from moment to moment, by a living God—if, in the great phrase of the Epistle to the Hebrews, He *upholds all things by the word of His power*—He can bring about what He wills without any interference or intervention at all. The whole of this difficulty as to miracle arises, in fact, from a kind of Deism which shuts God out of the universe He has created, and enthrones a sort of automatic destiny in His place. It supposes that God has had nothing to do with the world since the creation except to interfere with the mechanism now and again in order to work a miracle.[2] It is difficult to believe that any such fantastic cosmogony was ever seriously held by anyone who had thought it out, but there is no doubt at all that this kind of half-realized theory of the working of the universe is behind all arguments that turn upon the notion of intervention or interference by God. Here are two examples of this fallacy, from the writings of two very able and very thoughtful men, which I have chanced upon in my reading lately. Writing of miracle August Sabatier says that he could not accept it if it means " either the suspension or the subversion of the laws of nature, or the intervention of the First Cause in certain particular cases ".[3] And writing of providence George Tyrrell says that he is dubious as to what is and what is not providential, since " if Providence had been disposed to upset the established order of things in favour of my valuable soul, I cannot understand why the intervention was not earlier and more effectual—as judged by common sense ".[4] Now one is not much surprised to find this sort of thing in the newspapers, whenever there is a controversy about praying for rain, and in the street, whenever a secularist is arguing about miracle. But it is really surprising to find it in the books of thoughtful writers. For the whole conception of " suspending or subverting the laws of nature ", and " upsetting the established order or things ", by way of " the intervention of the First Cause ", proceeds upon pure assumptions, which, it is hardly too much to say, are demonstrably false. It assumes, first, that the order in which things happen is a predestined order, so that nothing can happen naturally otherwise than it does; and second, that this is an order with which God has had nothing to do since the creation. It is simply assumed that any and every future event *must* happen precisely in the particular way it does, and precisely then and there. Then we are asked, Will God intervene, interfere, upset the natural order, work a miracle, to make something else happen instead ? The answer is that there is no *must* about it. It is not predestined in an automatic, fixed, and necessary order

[2] *Cf.* Augustine, in *Joan. Evang. Tract,* II. 10.

[3] *Life of St. Francis of Assisi,* p. 433.

[4] *Autobiography,* I, p. 116.

that the thing *must* happen then and there, and in that precise fashion, and there is no need for God to interfere, if He is really directing what happens all the time.

There must be a universal system of causation and order and law, and everything that happens must have a regular place in it. If there is a God, and if He is in control of the universe and of all that happens in it, there is no need at any point to assert an " interference " on His part. The exceptional character of a miracle, if there ever is such a thing, cannot relate to the universal order; it can only relate to some partial experience and some partial knowledge of the universal order.[5] The limited knowledge which is alone possible to us consists mainly in recognizing that all things constitute a regular system, and in recognizing the place of any particular thing in that system. That is really what we mean by understanding anything. Suppose that something happens which is quite unparalleled in my experience. I never doubt for a moment that this new and puzzling thing belongs to a general system of existence in which everything is interlocked. I never dream for an instant that here is something which is without any cause, and without any relation to anything else in the universe. No sane mind could think that. I conclude that here is something which has a cause, and a regular relation to everything else in the universe, but I do not know what the cause is, and I cannot

[5] Dr. F. R. Tennant's little volume on *Miracle and its Philosophical Presuppositions* is probably the ablest book on the subject that has appeared in our generation, and much of it is extremely valuable. But it seems to me that the conclusions and many of the arguments of the book are really vitiated because Dr. Tennant will not accept the view of miracle as relative, since then it would be only *mirabile* and not *miraculum*, to use his own phrase. His thesis is that a miracle, if it really is to be a miracle, must have an absolute character. But how can a miracle be absolute? I contend that a miracle which would always be a miracle, in every age, to every level of intelligence, to infinite knowledge as well as to finite knowledge, to God as well as to men, is strictly unthinkable. An *absolute* abnormality is inconceivable. Everything that is must finally fall within a total system of related being, and therefore be normal as seen in relation to that total system. It may stand outside, or appear to stand outside, some partial system, or some system partially known, but it cannot stand outside the total system as totally known. It *must* be relative to some partial experience or some partial knowledge.

imagine what the relation is. If my knowledge is enlarged, and I can begin to see what the cause of this unknown phenomenon is, and how it is related to all the other phenomena of the universe, I say that now I begin to understand it. That means that I see it falling into its place in the regular system of things. If the thing which is strange and unique should then proceed to happen again and again it is still more evident that it has a regular place in the system of things, and I am still more convinced that I understand it, in that sense of placing it among the regular sequences of cause and effect in the universe, the ordered system of existence.

But our minds are so constituted that when anything happens repeatedly and regularly, and we become used to it, we forget the wonder of it. Everyone knows how true that is, and indeed it has a marked bearing on the aesthetic side of human life. Every poet is a man who can discern the wonder of things: he has the childlike spirit that sees the marvellousness of the ordinary. The child has that spirit of wonder because he is new to the world, and all things are strange to him, but as he grows older the light that never was on sea or land fades into the common light of day. The poet has recovered, or he has never lost, that childlike wonder, and he can see, and express, the splendid strangeness of the world. But for most of us the wonder is lost in our prosaic familiarity with what we see and hear and know. Any effort in the way of intellectual detachment, anything that breaks the spell of familiarity, brings the wonder back.

One has only to think of a universe organized on different lines to this universe to see that the most familiar things are really wonderful, and that what seem the most wonderful things to us would speedily lose their wonder if they became familiar. Thus there is nothing more intrinsically wonderful in the resurrection of a dead man than in the birth of a child; indeed, the intrinsic marvel would be less, for it is really less wonderful for a life that has existed to be revived than for a new life to come into existence.[6] The whole difference lies

[6] Augustine, *In Joan. Evang. Tract* 8, 1. Compare also a passage from Paley's *Evidences of Christianity*, p. 302: "Abstractedly considered, that is,

in the regular recurrence of an event, which we call natural simply and solely because the regular recurrence of it has made us familiar with it. That is unchallengeable, if you think it out. If this were a world in which men rose from the dead every day, but in which it was alleged only once or twice in history that a child had been born (and many people were doubtful as to whether that event had ever happened at all) we should regard the birth of a child as a miracle and the resurrection of a dead man as a most ordinary event. Our mere unfamiliarity with the fact of birth would make us see the wonder of it, and we should call it miraculous. Our mere familiarity with the fact of resurrection would blind us to the wonder of it, and we should call it natural.

It hardly need be said that every single thing in the world is wonderful, and equally wonderful, to the mind that can contemplate it with a real detachment. If we use the word miracle loosely and mean merely a wonder (though etymologically, of course, that is what *miraculum* means) everything in the universe is miraculous, and the universe itself is the supreme miracle. For the greatest wonder of all is not that there should be any apparent exception to the general system, but that there should be a system at all. As Mr. Chesterton once characteristically remarked, the really wonderful thing is not that the pumpkin should change into a coach-and-six, as it does in the fairy tale, but " that the pumpkin should go on being a pumpkin ". The persistence of things is a greater wonder to a thinking mind than the change of things, and there cannot be the one without the other. When we say that anything changes, we mean that there is *some thing*, still in some way the *same thing*, which changes, and unless that thing in some way remained the same thing it could not change, for there would be nothing to change. The changing and the unchanging are

considered without relation to the difference which habit, and merely habit, produces in our faculties and modes of apprehension, I do not see anything more in the resurrection of a dead man than in the conception of a child." I suppose one is expected to apologize for even mentioning Paley to-day, but I have never forgotten the above sentence since I first read it as a boy, sixty years ago.

correlatives: change could not come to pass without permanence. But the superficial mind is more impressed by the change, and the profounder mind is more impressed by the permanence. The greatest wonder of all is that there should be a universe which persists in being, and that it should *be* a universe, an ordered, coherent, related unity of existence. But we are used to the permanence and regularity of the universe, and accept this as the usual, ordinary, and (as we say) natural state of things, merely because we are used to it. As Pascal profoundly said, *J'ai grand peur que cette nature ne soit elle-même qu'une première coutume, comme la coutume est une seconde nature.*[7] The habit of familiarity has the same effect in respect of all the normal events which come to pass within the universe. For what happens repeatedly and regularly fails to create the sense of wonder in an unthinking man, simply because it does happen repeatedly and regularly, and his senses and his mind become accustomed to it. If the sun and moon and stars suddenly appeared to men for the first time in the history of the world, that would be a stupendous miracle.[8] But because the sun rises and sets every day, and the moon waxes and wanes every month, and the stars appear night by night, we forget the astonishing strangeness of it all. We call it natural, and forget to wonder at it, merely because it all happens again and again, and at more or less regular intervals. Anything, absolutely anything, that can happen in this universe would be a miracle if it only happened once, because then the wonder of it would be forced upon our minds. And anything, absolutely anything,

[7] *Pensées* (93), p. 39 : " I am greatly afraid that nature itself may be only first custom, as custom is second nature."

[8] Lucretius, *De rerum Natura*, II, 1032-35.

> Omnia quae nunc si primum mortalibus extent,
> Ex improviso si sint objecta repente,
> Quid magis his rebus poterat mirabile dici,
> Aut minus ante quod auderent fore credere gentes ?

(" All these, if now they were to come to being for the first time for mortals, if all unforeseen they were in a moment placed before their eyes, what story could be told more marvellous than these things, or what that the nations would less dare to believe beforehand ? ")

that can happen in this universe would cease to be a miracle if it happened repeatedly and regularly, because then the mere recurrence of it would familiarize us with the fact, and we should forget the wonder of it. In this sense it is strictly true to say that the whole difficulty about the miraculous is psychological. It does not lie in the structure of external nature; it lies in the structure of the human mind, which is such that the mere repetition of an experience blinds us to the fundamental wonder of it, unless we are children, or poets, or philosophers, or believers. When we have in some measure the naïve mind of the child, or the sensitive mind of the poet, the detached outlook of the philosopher, or the faith of the disciple, the strangeness of life and the world is always with us, and when we know that we live in a universe of miracle, we are not so ready to deny a wonder merely because it is a wonder.

The loss of the sense of wonder arises mainly from our familiarity with the thing, but partly also from our familiarity with the name of the thing—the mere conventionality of the phrases used to describe it. The modern child is familiar with the electric light in the house, and with the aeroplane in the sky: all his life he has known both the things and the names, but the lost wonder of these modern marvels might be brought home to him by nothing more than a change of descriptive phrases. Suppose you told him a strange tale about a sorcerer who seized a flash of lightning, and fastened it up in a crystal globe to serve him as a lantern, or about another wizard who made a kind of bird out of wood and wire and canvas, and then compelled it to fly by setting fire to some oil in its brazen heart. Both these stories, which sound so mythical, are not untrue descriptions of the electric light and of the aeroplane, given in unfamiliar terms, and it is perhaps worth observing that they are the only terms that would have been possible to some man in the Middle Ages, if he could have encountered the modern inventions, and if he had been compelled to describe them. Here it is a question of the familiar character of a descriptive phrase helping to accentuate the familiarity of the fact, and the unusual character of a descriptive phrase helping to reveal the strangeness of the fact. But whether the wonder is disguised in part by a mere conventionality of phrases, or, as is always the ultimate fact, by a mere familiarity of general experience, it remains true that the most ordinary thing in the world would be a miracle to us if it only happened once, and that the most fantastic, amazing, and supernatural thing we can imagine would cease to be a miracle to us if it happened constantly. The wonder is always there for the man who can see it, and the believer who has experience of strange guidance in his own life, and of strange answers to his own supplications, is the more ready to believe in the strange and supernatural events that we call miracles.

VIII

THE MIRACLES OF CHRIST

VIII

THE MIRACLES OF CHRIST

As has been already suggested, religion is concerned with the supernatural, not merely because of miracles, strictly so called, but because of the way that the supernatural enters into the experience of providence and of prayer. The religious interest in miracle as such, however, is mainly centred in the miracles of our Lord. That is not to say that the miracles recorded in the Old Testament, or in the Acts of the Apostles, are merely to be surrendered, but that the miracles said to have been wrought by Christ have a unique importance, as associated with what we believe to be the central fact of religion, the manifestation of God in the flesh. If those miracles did not happen, it does not matter much whether other miracles did or did not : if they did happen, the possibility (at the very least) of other miracles cannot well be denied.

The miracles of our Lord have been attacked repeatedly, in modern times, from one angle after another, but always with some thought in the mind of the critic that miracles are incredible and impossible because of the regularity of natural laws, of which any miracle is supposed to be a breach. It is suggestive to notice that the unspoken (and often unrealized) implication here is that this infraction of natural laws is always a supposed infraction of those laws *as far as they were known and understood at the period when the criticism was advanced*, and no allowance was ever made for the possibility that the miracle might be due to the operation of laws as yet unknown, and therefore might not involve a breach of law at all. This is illustrated by the changed attitude of the sceptic toward the miraculous cures related in the Gospels. Two or three generations ago the attack upon the supernatural simply denied every miracle in the life of our Lord. No distinction was made between miracles of healing and the rest.

Now almost every critic will admit that probably the miracles of healing (using the word miracles here without prejudice) really happened. It is important to note the way in which this change of mind has come about. A good deal more is known about suggestion, hypnosis, morbid psychology, and the relation between the mind and the body generally, than was known in the past, and many cases of abnormal cures have been investigated. Consequently, men of science think they can begin to see a rationale of such cures, and they are ready to admit them as facts. There has been no change in the realities of the situation: it is only that the facts have been more carefully investigated, and are beginning to be understood. There was ample evidence of abnormal cases of healing in the lives of the saints, and in the history of revivals of religion, and probably everyone who has had any wide experience of pastoral work has come across examples of such strange facts. The facts are there, and always were there, but in the past they were simply ignored, or regarded as mere superstition, unworthy of serious scientific investigation, and so, in a purely doctrinaire fashion, denied outright. Now they are closely investigated, partly understood, and admitted to be facts. It ought to be said, and said plainly, that all this does not represent a scientific temper of mind. To deny the existence of facts in this cavalier fashion, because you have not bothered to investigate them, and because you do not understand them, and therefore declare that they are impossible, is a procedure that is neither intelligent nor honest. There are more things in heaven and earth than are dreamt of in our philosophy, and the really scientific attitude is to keep open a vista for what are as yet inexplicable events.

But the scientific sceptic who fifty years ago flatly denied, and to-day admits, the miracles of healing, would still flatly deny the rest of the miracles. What if something happens with these parallel to what has happened in the case of the miraculous cures? The phenomenon of levitation has been recorded again and again in the lives of mediaeval saints, and in some religious revivals in modern times, as well as in the *séances* of so-called spiritualism. In many of these instances, it seems difficult for any candid mind to deny the alleged fact. I have come across one or two recorded examples of levitation during religious revivals in this country where the evidence (in some cases of persons still or lately surviving) is such as I personally could not refuse to accept. Yet all this has been either contemptuously denied or disregarded by most men of science. If this particular phenomenon is observed and investigated in the future, and some high-sounding phrase is devised to describe the supposed law which governs it—psychoanokinesis, let us say—the scientists will begin to admit the fact. If that comes to pass, it will be at last grudgingly allowed that possibly the story of our Lord's walking upon the water is a record of what really happened. The history of modern thought has many examples of this kind of doctrinaire disbelief reluctantly yielding to the logic of facts, in the light of later investigation and later discovery. It is always being assumed, in the cruder attacks upon the supernatural, that modern times have seen the irrational credulity of theologians repeatedly exposed by scientific progress; it would be at least equally true to say that scientific progress has repeatedly exposed the irrational incredulity of scientists. A really rational attitude of mind will always remember that our knowledge is limited, that the frontiers of discovery are always being pushed forward, and that there are a good many things on which it is wise to keep an open mind.

If we are prepared to do that, there are some facts about the miracles related in the Gospels which differentiate these from such other marvels as we should merely dismiss at sight, and which give them a striking look of verisimilitude. One of these is what may be described as the total absence of any note of extravagance or fantasy. There is no miracle attributed to our Lord, for example, that demands a belief in the existence of any fact that is absolutely unknown to men, or absolutely contrary to nature, as it were : one of the most striking features of the miracles of the New Testament is that they all move within the range of nature, to speak paradoxically. They may describe as happening in a moment what in the world of nature happens only in a lengthy process, or as happening because of a word or a touch what in the world of nature happens only as the result of a whole series of organic causes, but they are all, in a way, events which really happen within the world of nature, though they usually happen along other lines. The sick are sometimes healed, the blind do sometimes recover their sight, the dead are even sometimes resuscitated in these days, but it is by medical treatment; the bread is multiplied every year to feed the multitude, but it is by a process of growth in which the harvest is thirty or sixty or a hundred-fold of the seed sown; the water does every year become wine, but it is by a process of growth in which the rain falling into the soil becomes the sap of the vine and the juice of the grape. The miracles which are paralleled here are not unnatural events in the strict sense of the word: they are not happenings that lie altogether outside the bounds of our experience of nature; rather they are things that do happen in nature, but happen there in another way, through a regular process which we call natural. All the miracles of our Lord are aligned with the natural process, though they stand out vertically, so to speak, as exceptions to it, because of their mode; and this characteristic seems to me an important and impressive fact. One has only to think of the miracles in the apocryphal gospels and in the legends of the saints, to remember many examples of what is merely puerile and merely fantastic. Thus Jesus in His boyhood is said to have made sparrows of clay, and then clapped His hands, whereupon they came to life and flew away; and it is related of one of the mediaeval saints that he used to hang up his cloak on a sunbeam! Contrast such fanciful marvels as these with the miracles in the New Testament which are all, as I have suggested, along the general line of what may be called natural possibility. They are not *un*natural, even if they are *super*natural. They do not, as it were, traverse the natural, even if they transcend it. They are more like some strange intensification of a natural process than like a mere abolition of it. They are not mere marvels, the whole quality of which consists in a bare contradiction of the natural.

It is perhaps significant that τέρας, "wonder" is never used in the Synoptics, in our Lord's own discourses, of His own miracles, but only of the miracles of "false Christs" and "false prophets". His own deeds are never described or thought of by Himself as mere marvels. The word used is always σημεῖον or δύναμις, "sign", or "power". His miraculous deeds are never those of a mere thaumaturge, for they always have a moral and spiritual quality. They are either "powers", done for the actual relief of need or suffering, or "signs" given to teach some spiritual lesson in a vivid and memorable way. That is to say, they are precisely what might be expected of One whose business in life was to do deeds of wonderful mercy and to teach lessons of wonderful truth, and who possessed gifts which enabled Him to do these things more wonderfully than any other man who ever lived.

Then it is never to be forgotten that Christ Himself is "the miracle of miracles", as St. Thomas Aquinas said, and that we believe in the lesser miracles ultimately because we believe in Him Who was the greatest miracle of all. That the personality of our Lord was miraculous is true from every angle, but most strikingly of all in respect of His sinlessness. It may be taken as a spiritual canon of universal validity that the more saintly a man is the more he is aware of his own sinfulness and selfishness, the less he thinks of himself, the less he claims for himself, and the more humble and penitent he is, growing in humility and in penitence as he grows in goodness. There can be no question of the truth of this. It stands out as perhaps the main characteristic of all sanctity. But in our Lord all that is absolutely reversed. He has no sense of sin; He never betrays a spirit of contrition; and He makes the most absolute and imperious demands for Himself, declaring that we must be ready to abandon all things for His sake. Where the mark of greatness in every other religious teacher is that he keeps himself in the background, and asks our acceptance only of the message that he brings, Christ always places Himself in the forefront of all that He has to say—*Come unto Me! Believe in Me! Follow Me!* In any other this would be the most demented egotism: in Him it is natural and inevitable. No other man in the history of the world has dared to assume such a place, and to make such a demand, but we dare not challenge what He does and what He requires, if once we know Him, and know ourselves. He is the moral miracle of all history and all humanity.

We do not believe in Christ because of the miraculous deeds He is said to have done. We believe in His miracles because we believe in Him, and we know Him to be the supreme miracle. If we did not believe in Him as a unique personality we should not trouble ourselves for a moment about the marvels He is said to have wrought. As a matter of fact no one believes in miracles at all except along the track, as we may say, of extraordinary personalities and of extraordinary conditions. The most credulous person does not believe that miracles happen at any time and under any circumstances. The orthodox Christian believes that miracles did happen along the main line of revelation, in the religious experience of Israel and in the life of our Lord and of His apostles; and some of us believe that they still happen, in the lives of the saints, and in periods of spiritual intensity such as the greater religious revivals. Here is a limitation not to be forgotten, for it means that the miraculous occurs, if it does occur, where the personal and psychological factors are of the most extraordinary kind—that is to say, where unusual conditions make unusual events most likely and most credible. It is surely not unreasonable to believe that experiences and events that do not happen as a rule in the life of an ordinary man, at an ordinary time, may well have happened in the life of St. Francis of Assisi, or in the life of John Wesley, and under the spiritual conditions, intense, impassioned, and unusual as they were, of the Franciscan and the Methodist revivals in their earliest days. How much more reasonably may we believe that extraordinary facts may be found (and indeed that the believer would expect to find them) in the life of our Lord?

This is a point of the first importance, and yet it seems to be constantly forgotten in the discussion of the miracles of Christ. Much that would be almost incredible if it were related of any other person is credible enough when it is related of Him. Any rational believer will cheerfully admit that he would not take very seriously a series of marvels attributed, at a much later date, to one who was merely a religious teacher of the first century, and indeed that he would probably dismiss them at once as mere legend. That, by the way, is an impossible solution in the case of the miracles of Christ, for the simple reason that legend requires a fairly long time to grow. We may think readily enough of legend if there are two or three intervening centuries between the life and the record, but not very easily where the earliest record dates from within forty years or so of the event—a lapse of time well within one man's memory. The point at the moment, however, is that those who believe in the miracles of our Lord do so, first and last, because they believe in Him, and believe in Him as a unique personality. It is hardly too much to say that to most real believers the miracles of our Lord seem the natural appanage of His personality. They are articulated, so to speak, into His character and His life, and we believe they happened because He was what He was, and because they are so consonant with what He was. It is not only that you cannot excise the miracles without tearing the Gospels to tatters. It is that the signs that our Lord wrought are seen, when once they have happened, to be what we should expect from Him, when once we know Him to be what He was. If He really was the pure and perfect man, and more than man, it is surely to be expected that He would possess more than the normal powers and more than the normal knowledge of men, and that He would use His superhuman gifts naturally, as it were, in the fulfilment of His great mission. There is no sort of special pleading in this contention. We all believe extraordinary things of extraordinary men in some degree. If a man proves himself to be a superman we are prepared to believe in the record of his superhuman exploits, though they would have been incredible before they happened. Suppose that an author in 1750 had written a romance about an imaginary lieutenant of artillery in the French army who rose to supreme power, who defeated nearly every army and shook nearly every throne in Europe, who became Emperor of France, and at the height of his power dominated practically the whole of the Continent, who commanded the enthusiastic loyalty of millions of men, and who left his mark upon the history of the world for centuries to come—if all this had been related in a romance of 1750 it would have seemed wildly incredible. No one would have believed for a moment that such a career was possible. Yet it all happened, and it happened because Napoleon was a very extraordinary man. What would be fantastically incredible if it were attributed to any ordinary person, or any imaginary person, is credible enough when it has actually come to pass in the life of a real and extraordinary personage. It is because, on any reckoning whatever, our Lord was the most amazing personage in the history of mankind, that we believe He did amazing things. It is His own uniqueness that enables us, nay, as I believe, compels us, to believe in His unique deeds. Moreover, it is not merely that all this belongs to the past. It is that our Lord is still accomplishing the almost incredible in our own day, as through the ages of the past. For anyone who has any actual experience of religion in his own life and in the lives of other men, it is a fact not to be doubted that the strangest things that can be conceived are still being wrought in the name of Christ and by His presence and power. In every experience of sudden conversion, of answered prayer, and of the actual guidance of God in human life, there is a strain of what is strictly and properly the supernatural, and it is always associated with our Lord.

It is here that we encounter the greatest miracle in the life of Christ—His resurrection from the dead. In the actual experience of the believer He is always the living Lord: not a mere memory, or a mere influence, but a living Personality. So it is to-day, and so it has been through all the centuries past, and so it was at the beginning. It was not the surviving memory of a tragic martyr, or the surviving influence of a great teacher, that made early Christianity. It was the assured belief that *He who was dead is alive again, alive for evermore!* Can the Christian faith be explained by anything else? It was a moral and spiritual revolution that changed the world and everything in the world; it is unquestionably the greatest fact in the history of humanity; it has been the source of all that is finest in art and in literature as well as in religion; and it has been the inspiration of the noblest thought and the noblest endeavour that has ever been found amongst men—did all this originate from a mere delusion? the false belief that a dead man had risen from the dead? Surely that is the most insolent and destructive anomaly that was ever presented to a rational mind! Is there a single example in the history of the world where such tremendous and beneficent consequences, reaching through the ages, and affecting the life of humanity in a thousand ways, were brought about by a mad credence in a thing that never happened? Something unique *did* happen, something unique *must* have happened, that was a sufficient cause for the amazing results that followed, and the only rational explanation is that what happened was what the disciples believed.

It is considerations of a somewhat similar kind in their application to earlier ages that make one hesitate to deny, as easily as some do, the miraculous element in the Old Testament. For here again there is the element of the unique, though now it is not a unique personality, but a unique nation. Whatever his beliefs about the supernatural might be any honest thinker would surely admit that the experience of Israel represents far and away the highest level of religious attainment in the world before the advent of Christ. The people of Israel were the pioneers and preceptors of the world in spiritual religion as definitely as the Greeks were in the intellectual sphere, and the Romans in the political realm. It is an amazing thing when you think of it in a detached way that one small and insignificant people, dwelling in a land about the size of Wales, a little nation not distinguished in the history of civilization or conquest, or in any other way but this, should have developed those magnificent intuitions of the spirit which find utterance in the Psalms and the Prophets, and should have lifted the original worship of a tribal fetish out of all its early crudity into a superb faith in the one, eternal, almighty, omniscient and omnipresent God—the thought of God that has dominated religion ever since, and that is still the only conception of Deity that the mind of man will tolerate, either to believe it, or to deny it. As Renan said, the religious history of Israel is a miracle, in its own way. Is it irrational to believe, when there is this astonishing line of spiritual discovery (or of spiritual revelation, whichever you like to call it) reaching through the history of the people of God, and culminating in Christ, that there should be an aura of the supernatural accompanying it all the way?

The very fact that our Lord is the climax of a long history of revelation is in itself enough to remind us of another consideration that is not without importance. It may be reverently said that we could not think of our Lord's earthly life as coming at any other time The long ages of revelation to the chosen people had gone before, the intellectual dominance of Greece and the political dominance of Rome had prepared a world which was, in a sense, spiritually ready for the message of the Gospel and practically ready for the progress of the Gospel. It was in the fullness of the time—*τὸ πλήρωμα τοῦ χρόνου*—as the Apostle says, that God sent forth His Son, and the earthly life of our Lord, with all that accompanied it, fits into the course of the world's history then as it could not have done at any other period. It was the dawn of a new day, and that is not to be forgotten. We believe in our Lord's miracles, not merely as the unique deeds of a unique personality, but as set in a destined age, and happening at a unique moment in history. As some things are possible to-day that could not have happened then, so some things in the spiritual realm may well have happened then that would seem far from likely, and that perhaps are far from likely, to-day. The miracles of Christ stand out as unique events—except as a strain of the supernatural is found leading up to His advent and following from His presence and power in the lives of those who believe in Him. But it is to be remembered that those unparalleled deeds are associated with an unparalleled moment in the history of revelation, when an unparalleled Personality dwelt among men, and though that unique age is past and those unique deeds may not happen precisely as they did then, in the days of His flesh, the supernatural is still here in the believer's experience of providence and prayer, and it is always associated with Him Who wrought those strange deeds in the days of old.

IX

PROVIDENCE

IX

PROVIDENCE

It is scarcely too much to say that nearly all the difficulties about providence and prayer that beset the popular mind are due to the fallacy of taking a system of natural laws to mean a system of natural necessity. This derives from what has been called " the classical attempt of the nineteenth century to inflate empirical science into an equivalent to the obsolete *à priori* systems of the two preceding centuries ".[1] The " natural philosophers " of the seventeenth century, followed by the Deists of the eighteenth century, and the scientific materialists of the nineteenth century, assumed that the reign of law in the universe meant, and could only mean, that all things happened according to an immutable necessity, which, of course, simply amounts to the ancient notion of fate, ἀνάγκη. Such a conception means, logically, the end of all religion, for it is the denial not only of providence and of prayer, but of the freedom of the will, and ultimately of all morality. It is odd, however, that while some of these latter consequences are largely unrealized, the general thought of natural necessity subconsciously underlies most of the objections that are raised against providence, in particular. The classical expression of this in English literature is in the familiar lines of Pope :

> " Think we, like some weak prince, the Eternal Cause
> Prone for his favourites to reverse his laws ?
> When the loose mountain trembles from on high,
> Shall gravitation cease, if you go by ? " [2]

[1] Tennant, *Miracle and its Philosophical Presuppositions*, p. 14.

[2] *Essay on Man*, IV, pp. 121-8. The whole passage in Pope is borrowed from Wollaston. " If a good man be passing by an infirm building, just in the article of falling, can it be expected that God should suspend the force of gravitation till he is gone by, in order to his deliverance ; or can we think it would be increased, and the fall hastened if a bad man were there, only that he might be caught, crushed, and made an example ? If a man's safety should depend upon winds and rains, must new motions be imprest upon the atmosphere ? "—*Religion of Nature*, V, 18.

What is assumed here is manifestly that the mass of rock *must* fall precisely on that place, and precisely at that moment when you are passing that place, and that you *must* be passing that place precisely at that moment. Then it is triumphantly demanded if you expect a supernatural suspension of the law of gravitation to save you? The dilemma is presented as if it turned upon the invariability of natural law; it does not—it turns upon the pure assumption of a fixed fate. But there is no such fixity in events: we know that there is not. Because of continued rain, or hard frost, or a heavily laden wagon passing the place, or many other circumstances, the fall of rock may take place a little earlier or a little later. Or you may have mistaken the hour, so that you pass the place before or after you meant to do so, or you may be ill in bed, so that you cannot pass the place at all that day, and so on, almost endlessly. There are a thousand natural contingencies which, without ever going beyond the natural, may effectively prevent that particular event happening in the assumed way. If it be the will of God that I should not be crushed by the falling rock there is no need for a miraculous interposition to save me: the universal direction of events by the Divine providence within the natural order may accomplish that deliverance equally well.[3]

It is vital to religion to believe that there is such a direction of events—that the providential government and guidance of God exist and function in the world, and are facts in the experience of the believer. But while every religious man must believe that a Universal Will finally directs and rules all things in the universe, there are two very serious considerations to be remembered in connection with such a belief. One is concerned with the limitation of our knowledge; the other with the existence of evil.

It is obvious that human knowledge is very limited, and that we are quite unable to see more than a small part of the universal scheme. Consequently many things that look

[3] I have borrowed here, and at other points in the argument, some illustrations used in the essays on *The Theory of Miracle* and *The Problem of Prayer* in my *Studies in Religion*.

purposeless may really be, and indeed must be, actual elements in the purpose of God. If all that we could see of some great picture were absolutely restricted to one small corner of the canvas we should be totally unable to realize the significance and the splendour of the picture as a whole, even though we might discern the presence of some design and some beauty in the small portion of the picture that we could see. And so it must be on the universal scale. Let it be said emphatically that this is not special pleading : it is the obvious fact and the necessary truth. How could a finite mind possibly see and understand the whole of the infinite purpose of God ? That would be far more impossible than for a small child to understand the complexity of some abstruse argument in philosophy or some abstruse calculation in mathematics. It surely does not need to be argued that a limited intelligence operating within space and time cannot hope to understand fully the eternal purpose of the omniscient mind and the omnipotent will of the Most High.

Moreover, it is precisely this limitation of our knowledge that makes the sphere of faith, in the intellectual aspect of it. " We have but faith; we cannot know; for knowledge is of things we see." There would be no place for faith, in this sense, in a crystalline universe where there was no mystery, exactly as there will be no place for faith in the immortal life, when we know as also we are known. If we had that absolute understanding of the purposes of God here in this life religion would not be what it is, for the life of man would not be what it is. Our life is not lived in an atmosphere of perfect knowledge, but amid much darkness and ignorance and perplexity. Many things we do not know at all; many things we know very imperfectly; some things we know clearly and certainly enough to make them the guiding principles of our life. And it is this mixture of knowledge and ignorance that provides the sphere of hope and fear, of challenge and choice, of venture and faith, which constitutes so much of our moral and spiritual life. The very essence of religion, in this sense, is that it is a life of trust; we dare to believe in the supreme love of God even when we cannot possibly see how it is finally to be reconciled with some of the tragic elements of life.

The other fact to be remembered is the existence of evil. It is painfully plain that any consideration of the providence of God must sooner or later encounter that problem. For the question of the supernatural in any form is really concerned with the control that is exercised by God over the world which He has made. If there is a Deity, and if He is in real control of the universe, there can be no impossibility in believing that He guides our lives, that He answers our prayers, and that He can effect the wonders that we call miracles. But *is* God in complete control of the universe? There is a sense in which we must say that He is not, and this is not the conclusion of scepticism: it is the postulate of all religion. No doubt it is vital to religion to believe that at the beginning and at the end of the universe the will of God is dominant and absolute, but it is equally vital to religion to hold that there is a sense in which the will of God does not actively and absolutely rule all things here and now, everywhere and at all times. If it were so it would mean that God had expressly ordained all the sin and suffering of the world, and that all that is in the universe is exactly as God willed it to be—a mere Deistic fatalism which would make it impossible to believe in the goodness of God, and which would rule out moral responsibility as completely as it would rule out faith and prayer. But it is not the will of God alone that has determined all that is in the world, and to say that is merely the negative statement of what is positively meant, in part at least, by the freedom of man's will and by the fact of man's sin. I know, if I know anything at all, that I can sin—that is, that I can do the thing that God forbids me to do. It is the mere contradiction of the will of God, and yet it is a fact that He allows me to do it.[4] If we believe in God at all we must

[4] The older theologians distinguished different aspects of the Divine volition as the *creative* will of God, His *commanding* will, and His *permissive* will (*voluntas permissiva*), and this was more than an intellectual refinement, for if we believe in God in any real sense we are simply compelled to say that He permits what He does not command, and indeed that He permits the very contradiction of what He commands.

believe that He has delegated (and to that extent, as it were, resigned) some portion of His authority into the hands of men, that they might work out their own destiny.

We know, then, that the writ of the Almighty does not run everywhere in this world. The will of God is actually thwarted by the sin of man, for every act of sin means that a man does what God wills that he should not do. By His own decree, in the creation of man, the Most High has circumscribed His own range of action in the world. That is unquestionably true of the existence of man, and it must be equally true of the existence of any other being to whom the power of free-will and self-determination is given, if there are any such beings. We cannot therefore say that the will of God is immmediately effective everywhere and always in the world, and it is evident that here is a factor which may limit and cancel, to some extent, the action of God in regard both to providence and prayer. Doubtless it is profoundly true that, in the words of the Psalmist, He makes the wrath of man to praise Him, and that He weaves even the sins of men into the beneficent purpose of His providence. But it must also be true that the good purpose of God is sometimes prevented, perverted, or delayed, by human sin. The rule of God in this world must be such as might be illustrated, without any lack of reverence, by thinking of a wise and good king who rules over a realm in which there is a serious rebellion: it is not in every place and at every time that what the king commands is done. Would anyone who knows the mind of Christ dare to say, for instance, that a devastating war is according to the will of God? It is brought about solely by the folly and the wickedness of men. If men were what God wills they should be, and if they did what God wills they should do, the world would never see another battlefield. Manifestly there is much in this world for which man is responsible, and not God.

But is that all? It would seem that the entire element of cruelty and irrationality in the universe cannot be attributed to the moral perversity of man, for it is plain that some of it was in the universe before man came on the scene. At this point we encounter something of a gap in modern religious thought. For many years past, in reading many books dealing with religion and theology, one has frequently felt that there was something missing. It has been possible, perhaps, to agree with everything that was said, but there was something which has not been said, and which, in many cases, has apparently not been realized as a part of the religious issue at all. Many studies of the redeeming death of our Lord, for example, leave the impression that it has been difficult for the writers to discover any principle of real urgency in the Atonement. If you merely regard the human aspect of our Lord's Death it was a tragic martyrdom; it stands in line with every other martyr's death, and may be said to illustrate the sacrificial strain which runs through human history (though even then the element of sacrifice needs to be explained as an inevitable element of experience). But if you seek for some deeper and more elemental significance in the Cross, many theologians are only able to say that it is a final revelation of the love of God. That is, no doubt, a supreme fact, and a supreme truth, but is it all the truth? Did the uttermost revelation of the love of God *necessarily* take the form of an unspeakable tragedy, and why? It seems unsatisfying to think that the Cross of Christ was merely an exhibition, even though it was an exhibition of Eternal Love. In the range of human experience, at least (and that is all we have to go by, after all) we should think that there was something unreal, pretentious, and theatrical in a tragic display of love, unless there was some tragic necessity that made the agony inevitable. Where is that element in the Cross?—the superhuman and supernatural necessity that drove our Lord to Calvary and wrung out of His pure soul the anguished cry of dereliction at the last?

The same sense of a question unasked and unanswered forces itself upon you when you read many books that treat of the doctrine of sin. There has been a real advance, in some ways, in this particular field of theological thought, for our whole conception of sin is, or ought to be, much more adequately grounded in fact than of old, because we know so much more both of the psychology of the individual and of the history of the race. But this advance has left the particular issue here referred to absolutely untouched. For it simply does not matter, in this respect, whether you belong to the seventeenth century and take the legend of the Garden of Eden for literal history, or whether you belong to the twentieth century and think in terms of a long evolution of man from the lower animals. In each case the ulterior question remains. Why has the history of mankind involved, and inevitably involved, as it would appear, the fact of sin? Why is it necessary that man should have, in the very process of becoming what man is, and yet more in that of becoming what man ought to be, the experience (to put it at the least) of failure, of shame, of disunity, and of some elemental despair?

The same sense of a fundamental insufficiency makes itself felt in many attempts to deal with a doctrine of providence, when the issue has to be faced as to how the more tragic and irrational elements in the world, especially as they intrude into the experience of men, are to be reconciled with what we believe about the supreme goodness and the supreme power of the Almighty. What is it, in the last resort, that so strangely distorts or at least masks the love of God, and so terribly thwarts what we must believe to be His gracious purpose? Here is a little child who runs into the road after his ball and is mangled and killed by a passing vehicle. What are the possible attitudes to such a tragedy from the religious point of view? The mere pietist would say that it is the will of God; that we must not judge the Most High; and that in His eternal purposes what looks like evil is really good. The ordinary man who has less piety, and who esteems himself to have rather more common sense, while he really has no more intelligence than the pietist, would probably say that the tragedy was due to the working of natural laws, and that we cannot expect God to be continually interfering with the machinery of the universe.

Now consider what these positions really involve. There is a great truth in the pietist's contention, of course. If we believe in God at all we must believe that His ways are inscrutable, and that out of all the evil of the world a final purpose of good will be wrought. But while that must be true, it is really no satisfying answer to the problem of the immediate tragedy. The conclusion is too remote and too impersonal. It is like attempting to comfort a man who is dying of some agonizing disease by assuring him that a thousand years hence medical science will have abolished it. What of the relation of God to the immediate fact? I simply refuse to believe that the dreadful death of that little child, and the agony of its father and mother, is the act of God, or that it is according to the will of God, in any direct sense. And I think that every man who is really religious and really honest would agree—except in so far as we are concerned to safeguard what seems to be a vital belief in the omnipotence of God.

But suppose you say that the cruel and irrational facts of life are due to the relentless working of the mechanism of of nature, which is non-moral and non-intelligent. That, if you really mean it in all its implications, is the end of religion; it means the denial of God, or at least of any real activity of God either in the creation or the direction of the universe. If nature is a soulless mechanism, it is impossible to think of a God of eternal love, either as the Creator of it at the beginning or as in the continual control of it all throughout. There has been of late years an attempt to save the situation by holding a semi-Deistic doctrine, and it has been argued that Christian theism "must be sufficiently tinged with Deism to recognize a relatively settled order, and an order in which the causation is not immediate Divine creation".[5] That is to say, while God is the Creator, the creation is a sort of regular mechanism which God largely leaves to itself to run its appointed course. I cannot think that such a view will ever commend itself generally to the minds of men who wish to hold on, because of their own experience, as well as because of what they believe is involved in their faith in God, to a belief in the reality of prayer and of providence.

A poignant doubt as to the providential government of

[5] Tennant, *Miracle and its Philosophical Presuppositions*, p. 51.

God is suggested by occasional events which do look like the working of a mindless machine. When an earthquake or a volcanic eruption overwhelms many thousands of innocent people, with every circumstance of horror, it is a ready and apparently reasonable way of interpreting such an event to say that it is due to the relentless working of natural forces that are blind, and care not for the human disaster they have caused, since they neither know it, nor know themselves as the cause of it. It must be frankly confessed that there is a dreadful plausibility about this. It does look like that. But there are many questions that remain to be considered, if we too readily accept that explanation—as logically facile, at first sight, as it is difficult, on more serious consideration.

For what of all that is beneficent in the world? Are we to say that nature is both blindly benignant and blindly malignant? If we are consistent we must say that, and deny the existence of purpose anywhere in the universe. But if that be a true reading of the facts, how is it that nature chances to be so much more benignant than malignant? For the whole existence of human life and human happiness depends upon conditions that are benign, and if the disasters in the world are due to the blind mechanism of nature the favourable facts must be due to the same blind mechanism. How does it happen that a non-moral and non-intelligent mechanism produces results that are, upon the whole, vastly more rational than irrational, and vastly more kind than cruel?

Let us try to make a large induction, in a detached way, as to the general interpretation of existence. Upon any sane view the universe is a good universe, on the whole, but there is undeniably a bad streak in it. There is much more happiness than misery in the world, but there *is* misery; much more health than disease, but there *is* disease; much more goodness than sin, but there *is* sin. It looks like a benevolent and beneficent world, that has somehow got a malignant strain in it. It looks like a world made by a good God, but in which there is some primitive and puzzling defect. Both sides of this appear to be true. We feel that any desperate pessimism is an unbalanced and unjustified view, since it exaggerates the cruel and irrational element. We also feel that any easy optimism is equally an unbalanced and unwarranted view, since it ignores the factor of cruelty and irrationality. A sane philosophy, and still more a sane theology, must do justice to both series of facts—the preponderance of goodness and happiness which seems to be in accord with the main design of the universe, and also the presence of pain and misery, which seems to be a sinister perversion of the general design, and which is, in any case, a very terrible reality in universal existence. There is no denying that, as a matter of fact, on any frank interpretation of the universe. Whether we are theists or atheists, whether we have any theory of the universe or whether we have none, this would seem to be a fair reading of the facts.

When you pass from the general interpretation of the universe to the more specific region of religious thought and religious experience, there has to be a parallel recognition, if we are honest. The whole reality, the whole poignancy of the soul's life is involved in it. If sin is a mere superstition, or at any rate a very unimportant thing, as modern novelists would have us believe, then naturally there is no need for redemption, or indeed for religion. But if sin is a dreadful thing—and the awakened soul knows that it is—and if God had to do a dreadful deed to save men from their sins, then behind all this there must be some terrible and tremendous fact. As De Maistre said, " The republic of Ragusa does not declare war on the Sultan, nor that of Geneva on the Kings of France". What is this strange and appalling thing that has invaded the universe and declared war upon God ?

In the New Testament, and in the thought of the early Church, there was an element that has almost disappeared from modern thought, and it fitted into the gap which we have been considering. Whether it was a satisfactory conception or not, it supplied the missing factor here in what may be called a religious view of the world, and in a constructive scheme of theological thought. It may be said that it is impossible for us to hold it to-day, at least in the original form, but nothing else has taken its place. It is the conception of evil as a real, active, and personal fact in the universe. It is rather surprising to find how large a place this holds in the New Testament, when we come to look into it carefully.[6] In the life of our Lord Himself there is the central experience of the Temptation, as well as the belief in possession by demons, found on almost every page of the Gospels; and many references like those to the strong man armed, and the enemy who sowed the tares, and the evil one who snatches away what is sown in the heart; and many sayings like "How can Satan cast out Satan"? and "I beheld Satan fallen as lightning from heaven". In the writings of St. Paul, again, there are many passages like those which refer to the power of darkness; the prince of the power of the air; the principalities and the powers, the world-rulers of this darkness, the spiritual hosts of wickedness in the heavenly places; the mystery of lawlessness.

All this considerable element in the teaching of our Lord, and in the New Testament, and in the earlier faith of the Church, may be dismissed, and it frequently is dismissed, as a mere survival of crude, magical, mythological ways of thinking. It does not matter at the moment whether that is warrantable or not. The point is that if all this is dismissed, and nothing else is put in its place, there is a hiatus in our religious thought. A range of belief that did offer some kind of a rationale of what is really the irrational element in the universe has been discarded, and nothing else has been substituted for it. If this were deliberate, so to speak, and the Christian mind had definitely resigned itself to a frank and complete agnosticism on this issue, the position might be defensible. But that is scarcely what has happened. The problem has hardly been faced. We have given up one kind of explanation, without devising another, and without frankly admitting to ourselves the very ominous nature of the issue, whether any explanation of it can be found or not. But the fact remains, and it is the most appalling fact in the universe.

[6] See Matt. 12. 22; 13. 19; 13. 28; 13. 39. Mark 3. 23; 4. 15. Luke 10. 18; 11. 21. John 8. 44; 13. 27; 17. 15. Rom. 8. 38. II Cor. 12. 7. Eph. 2. 2; 6. 12. Col. 1. 13. II Thess. 2. 7-9. I Tim. 4. 1.

There is a large element of cruelty and irrationality in existence, and we cannot, we dare not, attribute it to the active will of God. That is not merely a mental dodge to save our belief in the omnipotence and the goodness of God, because there is actual warrant for such an attitude of mind in our own experience. I know, if I know anything at all, that I can sin against God—that is to say, that I can do the thing that denies, defies, foils, and cancels the will of God, and the Almighty lets this happen. There is no escape, if we retain a belief in God at all, from the position that the Most High allows what He does not will, in the proper sense of the word. A created will, in other words, does thwart the will of God.

So much every theist would admit, in some sense at any rate. Then some would go on to treat this as if it were a sufficient explanation of the whole problem. What is wrong with the world is due to the sin of man, and there is no need to go behind that or beyond it. But can it be held that this really faces the whole enigma? In Hebrew religion the existence of evil was regarded, on the one hand, as a mystery, and, on the other, it was attributed to human perversity. It has been well said that " the myth of the Fall makes the latter explanation too unqualifiedly in the sense that it derives all the inadequacies of nature from man's disobedience, a rather too sweeping acceptance of human responsibility for nature's ruthlessness and for the brevity and mortality of natural life ".[7] There is certainly a perverse and irrational strain in

[7] Reinhold Niebuhr, *An Interpretation of Christian Ethics*, p. 38. Compare a passage later in the book. " The world was not a perfect harmony even before human sin created confusion. The idea in Hebrew mythology that Satan is both a rebel against God and yet ultimately under His dominion, expresses the paradoxical fact that on the one hand evil is something more than the absence of order, and, on the other, that it depends upon order. There can be disorder only in an integrated world ; and the forces of disorder can be effective only if they are themselves ordered and integrated. Only a highly cohesive nation can offer a threat to the peace of the world. Thus the Devil is only possible in a world controlled by God and can be effective only if some of the potencies of the Divine are in him. Evil, in other words, is not the absence but the corruption of the good ; yet it is parasitic on the good. In such a mythical conception evil is more positive than in monistic philosophies, and more dependent upon the good than in religious and philosophical dualisms. The myth of the Fall is thus in harmony with the mixture

existence apart from man, and prior to man. It was not a perfect universe before man appeared. There was pain and strife and death from the earliest age of the world, long before man, in the geological ages of the " dragons of the prime, That tare each other in their slime ". It would indeed simplify the problem if you could attribute the whole evil of the universe to man, but quite obviously you cannot do that. Since evil in any ultimate sense must be of the will, it would seem that there is, apart from man, a malignant and maleficent will at work in the universe, such as is assumed in the New Testament.[8]

The whole question of the providence of God is therefore not a simple issue, as it would be if we could say that all things are directly ruled by the will of the Most High. We must say that the will of God is conditioned by the perverse will of man, and also, as it would appear, by another perverse will that is not merely human, though we must also believe that both human and superhuman evil are somehow wrought into the providential plan. This, it must be remembered, corresponds with the most certain facts of religious experience. Every man who has a real knowledge of God and a real experience of the grace of God is assured beyond all doubt, by the actual events of his own life, that in spite of all the evil that is in the world, the guidance of God is a reality ; that he is continually directed and delivered by a providence that

of profound pessimism and ultimate optimism which distinguishes prophetic religion from other forms of faith and other world-views. In the faith of prophetic religion existence is more certainly meaningful, its meaning is more definitely threatened by evil, and the triumph of good over evil is ultimately more certain than in alternative forms of religion."—*Ibid.* pp. 83-4.

[8] " Dogmatics must here, as in other places, be logically inconsequent in order to keep to the facts. In spite of the omnipotence of God, or rather indeed because of the omnipotence of God rightly understood, the concept of creation must not at this point be followed to the end of the line, but we must rather explain those possibilities—sin, evil, death, the Devil—as being such that we have to reckon most definitely with their actuality, while we are unable to describe their reality and character better than by forbearing to ask for the ground (*Begründung*) of their existence, either in the will of God the Creator, or with Marcion and the Manichaeans in the will of an evil anti-god (*eines bösen Gegengottes*). These possibilities are to be taken seriously as the *mysterium iniquitatis*."—Karl Barth, *Credo*, p. 36.

mysteriously encompasses him; and that frequently the evil that assails him—undeniably evil as it is—becomes a factor of good in his life. He can often say of the malignant misdeeds of men, for example, what Joseph said to his brethren, "Ye meant evil against me, but God meant it for good". And while he does not profess to understand all the mysteries of life, he is sure that the actual providence of God is a wonderful fact in the sphere of his own experience. It is not an exaggeration to say that. I am certain that almost every experienced Christian would declare that while he naturally cannot pretend to explain the whole of the providential plan in the world, nor the particular incidence of calamity in the lives of other men, he is certain of the guidance and guardianship of God in his own life, and also that this is linked up with his experience of prayer, and with the whole element of the supernatural in the way that God has made Himself known to men.

X

PRAYER

X

PRAYER

THERE can be little doubt that a serious debility in religious faith to-day is due to the fact that for more than a generation past religious teachers with timid minds have tried to make an illogical and impossible compromise with passing fashions of thought, from a false deference to what they regarded as scientific authority. They have had a confused notion that what is called the supernatural is discredited, and they have tried to save what they could out of the religious *débâcle.* They were convinced that a real Incarnation had become an impossible conception, but that we might venture to say that God is in all men, and that He was perhaps rather specially in Christ. They believed that a real Atonement was out of the question, but that we might still speak of the Cross as a great example of devotion and sacrifice. They thought that to be asked to believe in a real Resurrection was trying the modern mind much too high, but that we might still talk of Christ living again in minds made better by His influence. They felt that miracles must be given up altogether, of course. They concluded that prayer could no longer be regarded as having any real effect in the universe, but that it might still be defended as a kind of vague fellowship with the unseen, promoting a mood of resignation in our souls, and disposing us to accept events which neither prayer nor anything else could change in the slightest degree.[1]

[1] Schleiermacher is in many ways the greatest of modern theologians, but in this direction his influence has been really pernicious. As Dr. Mackintosh has written : " It hardly needs saying that Schleiermacher's view of prayer has no foundation in the teaching of Christ. Our Lord offered prayers which cannot be described as prayers of either pure gratitude or pure resignation ; if language has a meaning, they were petitions in which definite things were asked from God. . . . This is a point in personal religion at which the modern mind, only too faithful to Schleiermacher's lead, has been scared into dumb and sad acquiescence by a purely gratuitous dogma about ' the inflexible laws of nature '. It will only breathe freely once more when it has regained contact with Jesus' thought of the living God."—*Types of Modern Theology,* pp. 93-4.

Few things are more irritating than this kind of attempt at a partial salvage of the supposed wreck of faith, and we are perpetually meeting with it in the shallower sort of religious book. On this particular issue we are assured again and again that prayer is not asking God for anything, but that it is really a sort of exercise in communion and in submission. Now it is manifestly true that prayer is communion with God, and that it does involve a humble submission to His holy will. But to make prayer consist in these, and to rule out, or diminish as much as possible, the element of petition, involves a subtle unbelief which is also a subtle hypocrisy. It means that you do not believe that prayer really effects anything or changes anything (since, apparently, all that happens in the world is determined by a mysterious fate with which God has nothing to do) but that you are not prepared to confess frankly that prayer is useless, and so you try to make out a case for retaining it as a mere psychological factor, and an entirely subjective thing. That is what this brand of teaching really means. It reduces the whole life of prayer to a sort of auto-suggestion. I cannot conceal my contempt for that kind of scared apologetic, which is far less respectable than any honest scepticism. Does prayer really effect anything in the world of fact?—that is the question. It is about as certain as anything can be in this world that prayer will not long remain as a part of the religious life of men when once they begin to believe that it has no results outside of themselves; and when men cease to pray, religion is at an end.

A sort of compromise, which it is difficult to call anything but absurd, has been advanced by some apologists. It is implied that while prayer cannot change anything in the world of external nature, where the inevitability of natural law is the supposed difficulty, yet prayer may be effective somehow in the spiritual world. That is to say you split the universe into two halves, the natural and the spiritual, and then think of the natural world as ruled by inevitable laws, and of the spiritual world as ruled by—what? There is only one universe; if it is law anywhere it is law everywhere, and if the action of inevitable laws prevents prayer from having any real results in one half of the universe, it equally prevents prayer from having any real results in the other half of the universe.

There is an example of this irrational compromise, or something very like it, in a famous book by a distinguished philosopher and psychologist. "We have heard much talk of late against prayer, especially against prayers for better weather and for the recovery of sick people. As regards prayers for the sick, if any medical fact can be considered to stand firm, it is that in certain environments prayer may contribute to recovery, and should be encouraged as a therapeutic measure. Being a normal factor of moral health in the person, its omission would be deleterious. The case of the weather is different. Notwithstanding the recency of the opposite belief, everyone now knows that droughts and storms follow from physical antecedents, and that moral appeals cannot avert them." [2] That is to say, prayer as a moral factor may induce physical results, so that there is some connection between the moral and the physical, within human life at any rate. Nevertheless, the weather, because it is the result of physical antecedents, cannot be influenced by prayer. Is not illness also the result of physical antecedents? and why should not the moral and the physical be connected outside the human body as well as inside it? If the answer is that within the sphere of human life there is an active connection between the mental and moral, on the one hand, and the merely physical, on the other, is it to be assumed that there is no such connection in the wider universe? That, of course, is a mere denial of the existence and activity of God.

It is true enough that from a purely religious point of view, without any reference to natural law at all, we have a different attitude in our supplications as these are directed toward the physical or toward the spiritual. But that is not because the intelligent believer thinks that it is somehow more possible for our prayers to be answered in the one region than in the other. It is because when we pray for some material thing we cannot be sure that it is really good

[2] William James, *The Varieties of Religious Experience*, pp. 463-4.

for us that our prayer should be granted, however much we may desire it, and so we cannot be sure that our petition is in accordance with the will of the Most High. If a man prays, for example, that he may succeed in business, for all we know it may not be the will of God to grant that prayer, and it may not be for that man's real and eternal good that it should be granted. There is therefore always a question in the believer's mind in such petitions, and there must always be a reverent submission to the will of God. That must be so even in the most tragic hours of life, and even with respect to what we most deeply desire and most keenly dread. It was the most pure and perfect of men, and the Redeemer of mankind, who said in His deepest agony of prayer, " Let this cup pass away from me ; *nevertheless, not as I will, but as Thou wilt* ".

But when we pray for spiritual blessings we need not say that, because we know already that it is the will of God to hear our prayer, and to give us what we ask. There is no question in my mind as to whether I am really asking according to the will of God when I ask for grace and goodness, and beseech God to bless me with every spiritual blessing in Christ. That *is* according to the will of God, and I know that it is before I begin to pray.[3] Therefore I do not need to feel or to express a yielding to the unknown will of God. It is, and it must be, the will of God to give me moral and spiritual blessings: it may be, for all that I know, the will of God to withhold temporal blessings, and therefore in our petitions for these there must always be a question and a submission— " if it be Thy will ".

But when this is remembered, as it always ought to be remembered, it is still true that if God exists there cannot be anything irrational in believing that He can really hear and answer our prayers, whatever region of the universe our supplications concern. For the existence of God means that a supreme intelligence is in final control of all that happens in the universe. Any alternative to that belief, such as fate or chance, is merely irrational, when you consider what it really means.

[3] Cf. St. Thomas Aquinas, *Summa theol.*, II, 2. q. 83, a. 6.

What explanation of universal existence is possible? There are some general facts to guide us. For one thing, the universe is manifestly one system of existence. It is impossible to think otherwise. When pluralist philosophers, for example, write of a " multiverse " they are really conceding the point at issue, for it is *a* multiverse—that is to say, one system in which they are attempting, by the use of the word " multiverse " instead of " universe ", to stress the variety instead of stressing the unity. But however various, however contradictory even, it may be, the totality of existence *is* a totality; the whole of things *is* a whole; it is one system in which everything is related to everything else, and all is bound into a final unity. That must mean that the numberless causes in the universe are all ultimately grounded in one final cause, which is the cause of all, the *causa causarum*.

Now how is that to be conceived except as intelligent, purposive, moral, and ultimately personal? [4] We know nothing originally of any cause except as discerned by human intelligence in external existence, and controlled (to some extent) by human will in the sphere of our own activity. Then we extend this generalized conception of cause to all things, and make it the fundamental postulate of science. Obviously we could not know anything of causation except as our minds discover it when in action in the world, and as our wills direct it when in action in our own lives. Causes, therefore, are always controlled and operated by a personal intelligence, as far as we have any experience of controlling and operating them, and they are always discerned by a personal intelligence, even when they lie beyond our power to control and operate. What conceivable right have we to suppose that there is no personal intelligence concerned when

[4] " While it may be possible, setting out from mind to account for mechanism, it is impossible, setting out from mechanism to account for mind."—James Ward, *The Realm of Ends*, p. 18.

" Either Force stands before Thought, so that Thought is not the primitive reality, but the result and accident of blind Force ; or Thought stands before Force, so that blind Force is not the primitive reality, but the effluence of Thought ; or, finally, Thought and Force are, at bottom only one and the same thing, and differ only in our mind's conception of them."—Trendelenburg, *Beitrage zur Philosophie*, II, p. 10.

we reach the universal cause ? It is precisely like saying that there must be an intelligent and intelligible cause behind every separate detail of a vast machine, but that there is no need to presume that there is any intelligent or intelligible cause behind the whole mechanism.

Moreover, what is moral is always linked with intelligence and with volition in human personality and life and action, which is where we have our only actual experience of causation. Why should we deny the existence of moral volition on the largest scale of all ? We find a complex of personal intelligence, of moral will, and of actual causation in our own experience, which, after all, is everything that we have to guide us in a larger interpretation of the universe. What reason have we, when it comes to that larger interpretation, to subtract the intelligent, the moral, and the personal, and leave only a residuum of mere causation, which, so reduced, amounts to a bare and empty fatality ? There must be an ultimate source of what is rational, moral, and personal in the world and that infinitude of intelligence and righteousness and personality we call God.[5]

The unwillingness on the part of many thinkers to ascribe personality to God seems to be due to a dread of anthropomorphism, though it is obvious that every form of thought or speech that can be used in reference to the Deity, or in reference to any explanation of the universe, is inevitably anthropomorphic in its origin, and in its original limitations, for we have nothing but our human conceptions, derived from our human experience, which we can use in thinking of anything whatever. But when we reach the ultimate we can at least transcend the limits of these human conceptions, and insist that they are to be expanded to the utmost. This, of course, is the justification of the *theologia negativa*, and indeed of all the greater terms that are used in philosophy as well as in theology. We begin with a recognition of the limited and dependent character of all our human experience, and of all

[5] "The source of morality must be moral. The source of knowledge must be rational. If this is granted, you rule out Mechanism, you rule out Naturalism, you rule out Agnosticism, and a lofty form of Theism becomes, as I think, inevitable."—Balfour, *Theism and Humanism*, p. 250.

the facts of the universe as known in our human experience, and then we expand the finite into the infinite and the relative into the absolute. So, too, when we think of God as the omniscient, the omnipotent, the omnipresent. We begin with the human experience of knowledge and power and presence as limited, and then proceed to annul the human limits when we apply these conceptions to the Deity. But some minds seem curiously unwilling to do this when we speak of the personality of God. It is a rather narrow and limited conception of personality in such a connection that is always rejected, as when a famous philosopher refuses the thought of " a God that can say to Himself ' I ' as against you and me ".[6] It is no doubt true that one principal trait of human personality is the fact of the separateness of individual experience; that I am I, and not you, that you are you, and not me; and that each man is a separate centre of the universe to himself. But that, while characteristic of human personality, is really characteristic of its defectiveness rather than of its essence. The more knowledge and experience I have, and the less there is from which I am separate, the more I really deserve to be called a personality, for then my personality is all the richer and fuller and more inclusive. Surely a perfect personality would be one with universal knowledge and universal experience ; one from which nothing was really separate, and from which nothing was really excluded; nothing, at least, that could be called positive existence. The perfection of personality must mean " One for whom there is no essential not-self, because all essential experience is His own ; an infinite fullness or Pleroma, in the language of St. Paul"[7]. Thus it is really God, and God alone, Who can say " I " in the absolute sense. All human personality must be a limited and defective transcript of the limitless and perfect personality of God. If it be said that this last is not personality, or is more than personality, the answer is that it is related to the personality we know as omniscience is related to the knowledge we

[6] Bradley, *Essays in Truth and Reality*, p. 432.
[7] J. R. Illingworth, *Divine Transcendence*, p. 21.

possess, and as omnipotence is related to the power we exercise. Call it omnipersonality, if you will, or super-personality, but do not forget (as some seem to do who use the latter phrase) that the super-personal means *more* than personal, and not *less* than personal. It means that God is all that we mean by personal when we use the word of humanity —all that, and infinitely more.[8]

Now if a personal God exists and rules there can be no impossibility in our prayers being heard and answered. There is nothing whatever, in fact, in any really scientific knowledge of the world, that forbids us to believe in prayer exactly as the simplest piety does. The only real difficulties that beset the doctrine and the practice of prayer are moral and religious. They are the ignorance of man in the presence of the infinite wisdom of God, which prevents us from knowing why our prayers are not always effective, or why, at least, they do not always seem to be effective; the sin of man, which in the very nature of it is an actual and present defeat of the will of God; and that mystery of lawlessness in the universe which was a challenge to the rule of the Most High before man was in the world, and before the world was made.

It is not too much to say that within these inevitable limitations—all based upon facts which are religious facts, and not derived from any merely scientific considerations—every religious man knows that prayer is answered, and often answered in the most unexpected, unlikely, and apparently impossible ways. It is a matter of actual experience in the life of the believing soul. It cannot be tested or tabulated in

[8] Compare the words of Herbert Spencer: "Those who espouse this position assume that the choice is between personality and something lower than personality: whereas the choice is rather between personality and something that may be higher. Is it not possible that there is a mode of being as much transcending Intelligence and Will as these transcend mechanical motion? Doubtless we are totally unable to imagine any such higher mode of being. But that is not a reason for questioning its existence; it is rather the reverse." (*First Principles*, p. 80.) This concedes all that the theist demands. The "mode of being" of the Deity must transcend all our thoughts, but it cannot be less than personal; that is to say, it must be personal, with as much exaltation and expansion of personality as words can say or thought can conceive, and more.

any way that would convince the sceptic, for he could always argue that the most amazing answers to prayer were mere delusions or mere coincidences, but the man whose prayer is answered knows better. Probably every experienced believer is as sure as he is of his own existence that, on particular occasions in his life, his earnest prayer to God has been answered in a way that it was impossible for him to imagine beforehand, and that—until the event happened—it would have been impossible for him to believe.

But however strange and supernatural (in the proper sense of that word) the results of prayer may be, it is manifest that they must be in accordance with the laws and conditions of the spiritual life, which are a part of the ordered system of the whole universe. And it is possible to state some of those laws and conditions beyond any doubt. First, all prayer is morally conditioned. It must be sincere, and that sincerity has a relation both to the actual conduct of a man and to his mental mood. Obviously prayer is not sincere if a man's deeds contradict the spirit of his supplication. It is always the fervent prayer of a *righteous* man that avails much in its working—πολὺ ἰσχύει δέησις δικαίου ἐνεργουμένη[9]—a righteous man, at least in intention, for when a sinner really repents it means that he wants to be righteous, and wills to be righteous. Our prayer cannot be sincere if it involves anything inconsistent with the love of God and the love of man. There lies the answer to the absurd and abominable challenge which was put forth years ago, that the efficacy of prayer should be tested in the case of a dozen hospital patients diagnosed as incurable, by Christians praying for the recovery of the first six! It is not too much to say that there must have been some moral as well as mental obtuseness in any man who made such a suggestion, or countenanced it. How could there be any spiritual sincerity or spiritual reality in prayers like those? Any Christian and compassionate heart, once aware of the suffering of those sick folk, would instinctively pray that they might *all* be spared, if it were the heavenly will. Anything else would really

[9] *Epistle of James*, 5. 16.

mean praying that some of the sick might die—to convince an unbeliever who would probably not then be really convinced, and whose logical conviction on such grounds, even if it did come to pass, would have no religious value whatsoever.

There are other factors in the life of prayer beside those which have been described as moral conditions, and some of these spiritual principles may be readily discerned, if we take our Lord's teaching, and the actual experience of the believer, as a rule of guidance. Thus in the words of Christ, as recorded in the Gospels, there are two strains of teaching with regard to prayer that seem paradoxical and almost contradictory. It is plainly taught that God is willing to give every good gift to those who ask. "If ye, then, being evil, know how to give good gifts unto your children, how much more shall your Father who is in heaven give good things to them that ask Him?"[10] It must be so, for if the very nature of God is Love, He must be more ready to give than we are to ask. But, on the other hand, it is also plainly taught that we must pray as earnestly, as importunately, as desperately, as if God were unwilling, and as if we had to overcome His unwillingness by our persistency. That is the whole point of the great parables of prayer.[11] The unrighteous judge was pestered into doing justice to the widow, against his own intentions, by her sheer importunity, and the householder asleep at midnight was harassed into giving the loaves, in spite of his reluctance, because his unwelcome visitor would not be denied. The reconciliation of this apparent paradox is not very difficult, and it is one of the spiritual principles that rule the life of prayer. For, however willing God is to give His best gifts, it is simply true to say that they cannot be given to the unwilling and the unreceptive. The rain and the sunshine are indeed sent upon the righteous and the unrighteous alike, in the bounty of God; but the higher gifts of grace are never forced upon a reluctant or indifferent soul. There is always a deep sense of need and a strong desire lying at the heart of real supplication, and it is these which make it

[10] *Matt.* 7. 11. [11] *Luke* 18. 1-7 and 11. 5-8.

possible for God to bestow His best gifts upon us, and for us to receive them.[12] It is only when we really want those gifts that they can be given and received, and if we really want them we shall ask, and ask eagerly and earnestly, until they are bestowed. Here, indeed, is one of the actual tests of our religious sincerity. How much, for example, do we really want that holiness of heart, that sanctification of spirit, without which none shall see God? How much do we pray for it, how often, how earnestly, how persistently? That is the precise measure of our real desire for it, and therefore the precise degree in which it can be bestowed upon us.

There is therefore always an equation between the passion and the persistence of prayer, on the one hand, and the spiritual result on the other. That is manifest alike in the experience of the individual and in the united life of the Church. If such things could be measured we should find an equivalence between the intensity of supplication in the souls of believers, the spiritual pressure, so to speak, that exists in the religious atmosphere, and the spiritual results that follow in the lives of men. The life of every saint, and the history of every religious revival, will illustrate that law of the spiritual life: it is a kind of conservation of energy in the realm of the spirit.

The life of prayer is ruled by such principles as these, which are laws of the spiritual life, but there is nothing in the laws of the physical world which can interfere in any way with the action of prayer. I say again, at the end of this volume, as I said at the beginning of it—*there is absolutely no real reason whatever, in science or philosophy, or any other realm of human knowledge*, why we should not believe that God has revealed himself to men in a way that is more than natural; and that He can guide and guard us by His providence on our way through life; and that when we cry to Him in our need He can hear and answer our supplications.

[12] Dante, *Paradiso*, XX, 94-9.

INDEX